CULTURAL STUDIES

Volume 5   Number 3   October 1991

EDITORIAL STATEMENT

Cultural Studies seeks to foster more open analytic, critical and political conversations by encouraging people to push the dialogue into fresh, uncharted territory. It is devoted to understanding the specific ways cultural practices operate in everyday life and social formations. But it is also devoted to intervening in the processes by which the existing techniques, institutions and structures of power are reproduced, resisted and transformed. Although focused in some sense on culture, we understand the term inclusively rather than exclusively. We are interested in work that explores the relations between cultural practices and everyday life, economic relations, the material world, the State, and historical forces and contexts. The journal is not committed to any single theoretical or political position; rather, we assume that questions of power organized around differences of race, class, gender, sexuality, age, ethnicity, nationality, colonial relations, etc., are all necessary to an adequate analysis of the contemporary world. We assume as well that different questions, different contexts and different institutional positions may bring with them a wide range of critical practices and theoretical frameworks.

'Cultural studies' as a fluid set of critical practices has moved rapidly into the mainstream of contemporary intellectual and academic life in a variety of political, national and intellectual contexts. Those of us working in cultural studies find ourselves caught between the need to define and defend its specificity and the desire to resist closure of the ongoing history of cultural studies by any such act of definition. We would like to suggest that cultural studies is most vital politically and intellectually when it refuses to construct itself as a fixed or unified theoretical position that can move freely across historical and political contexts. Cultural studies is in fact constantly reconstructing itself in the light of changing historical projects and intellectual resources. It is propelled less by a theoretical agenda than by its desire to construct possibilities, both immediate and imaginary, out of historical circumstances; it seeks to give a better understanding of where we are so that we can create new historical contexts and formations which are based on more just principles of freedom, equality, and the distribution of wealth and power. But it is, at the same time, committed to the importance of the 'detour through theory' as the crucial moment of critical intellectual work. Moreover, cultural studies is always interdisciplinary; it does not seek to explain everything from a cultural point of view or to reduce reality to culture. Rather it attempts to explore the specific effects of cultural practices using whatever resources are intellectually and politically available and/or necessary. This is, of course, always partly determined by the form and place of its institutionalization. To this end, cultural studies is committed to the radically contextual, historically specific character not only of cultural practices but also of the production of knowledge within cultural studies itself. It assumes that history, including the history of critical thought, is never guaranteed in advance, that the relations and possibilities of social life and power are never necessarily stitched into place, once and for all. Recognizing that 'people make history in conditions not of their own making', it seeks to identify and examine those moments when people are manipulated and deceived as well as those moments when they are active, struggling and even resisting. In that sense cultural studies is committed to the popular as a cultural terrain and a political force.

Cultural Studies will publish essays covering a wide range of topics and styles. We hope to encourage significant intellectual and political experimentation, intervention and dialogue. At least half the issues will focus on special topics, often not traditionally associated with cultural studies. Occasionally, we will make space to present a body of work representing a specific national, ethnic or social tradition. Whenever possible, we intend to represent the truly international nature of contemporary work, without ignoring the significant differences that are the result of speaking from and to specific contexts. We invite articles, reviews, critiques, photographs and other forms of 'artistic' production, and suggestions for special issues. And we invite readers to comment on the strengths and weaknesses, not only of the project and progress of cultural studies, but of the project and progress of *Cultural Studies* as well.

* * *

Contributions should be sent to Professor Lawrence Grossberg, Dept. of Speech Communication, University of Illinois Urbana, 244 Lincoln Hall, 702 S. Wright St., Urbana, Ill. 61801, USA. They should be in duplicate and should conform to the reference system set out in the Notes for Contributors, available from the Editors or Publishers. They may take the form of articles of about 5000 words, of kites (short, provocative or exploratory pieces) of about 2000 words, or comments on cultural texts and events. Reviews, and books for review, should be sent to Dr Tim O'Sullivan, School of Arts, Leicester Polytechnic, P.O. Box 143, Leicester LE1 9EH.

THE MUSIC INDUSTRY IN A CHANGING WORLD

Will Straw and John Shepherd	Editors' note	vi
John Shepherd	INTRODUCTION	251
	ARTICLES	
Simon Frith	Anglo-America and its discontents	263
Paul Théberge	Musicians' magazines in the 1980s: the creation of a community and a consumer market	270
Paul Rutten	Local popular music on the national and international markets	294
Robert Wright	'Gimme Shelter': observations on cultural protectionism and the recording industry in Canada	306
Jody Berland	Free trade and Canadian music: level playing field or scorched earth	317
Reebee Garofalo	The internationalization of the US music industry and its impact on Canada	326
Sara Cohen	Popular music and urban regeneration: the music industries of Merseyside	332
Laurie Brown	Songs from the bush garden	347
Lawrence Grossberg	Rock, territorialization and power	358
Will Straw	Systems of articulation, logics of change: communities and scenes in popular music	368
	REVIEWS	
Patrice Fleck	Pornotopia?	389
John Frow	Face value?	393

WILL STRAW AND JOHN SHEPHERD

EDITORS' NOTE

The conference of which this special issue of *Cultural Studies* is the proceedings was organized and hosted by the Popular Music Workshop of Carleton University's Centre for Research on Culture and Society. The Co-ordinator of this Workshop is Paul Théberge.

The Centre was established in 1989 to carry out research in cultural analysis, with a particular emphasis on Canada. Drawing on faculty strengths within the Faculties of Arts and Social Sciences and the School of Architecture, the Centre is designed to provide a setting for collaborative work between scholars from different disciplines interested in furthering research on cultural practices and forms from within the Canadian context. The Centre also encourages the involvement of graduate students at Carleton and scholars from other institutions in its research activities. In providing opportunities for public debate on cultural practices and forms the Centre promotes the exchange of information and research between scholars, practitioners and administrators, and the representatives of organizations involved in the practice, production and regulation of culture. In fostering collaboration with similar centres in Africa, Australia, Europe and the United States, the Centre also brings a comparative perspective to bear on debates within Canada on cultural practices and forms.

The Centre engages in funded research, promotes conferences, symposia and public lectures, and provides scholarly publications consisting of the texts of public lectures, working papers, and special issues of journals.

Further information on the Centre, its membership, its publications and its subscription programmes, can be obtained by writing to: Director, CRCS, Carleton University, Room A929, Loeb Building, Ottawa, Ontario K1S 5B6, Canada.

Advertisements: Enquiries to David Polley, Routledge,
2 Park Square, Milton Park, Abingdon, Oxon, OX14 4RN

Transferred to Digital Printing 2004

Subscription Rates (calendar year only): UK individuals: £28; institutions £45; rest of the world: individuals £30; institutions £48; North America: individuals $50; institutions $74. All rates include postage. Subscriptions to: Subscriptions Department, Routledge, Cheriton House, North Way, Andover, Hants, SP10 5BE.

Single copies available on request.

ISSN 0950–2386

© Routledge, 1991

Typeset by Type Study, Scarborough

INTRODUCTION

JOHN SHEPHERD

This special issue of *Cultural Studies* consists of the proceedings of an international conference organized and hosted by the Centre for Research on Culture and Society at Carleton University in November 1990. The organization of a conference on 'The Music Industry in a Changing World' was suggested by two sets of events in 1989. First, for Canadians, there was the conclusion of the anticlimactic free trade affair – anticlimactic because efforts to initiate a meaningful national debate on the issues raised by the abolition of trade barriers between Canada and the USA essentially failed. The impending passing of free trade legislation created some heat during the Canadian Federal General Election of late 1988, but very little light. Free trade legislation, which for Canadians created a common market with the USA, went into effect at the dawn of 1989.

Secondly, there were the dramatic events in Eastern Europe of late 1989. Whatever political and ideological interpretations are put on these events, the demise of Stalinism and the consequent devaluing of socialism's currency in the public mind (both East and West) can hardly detract from the anticipation of the creation of a grander and more powerful European market in 1992. If 1989 becomes emblematic of 'the world triumph of capitalism', then 1992 will likely become emblematic of a changing power relationship between the expanded European and North American markets. While the USA remains willing to act as the world's policeman, it seems clear that it cannot alone support economically the exercise of its military might. Further, while the contents and formats of the United States' cultural industries remain as pervasive and as influential as ever (witness the attempts of the USA to enter the deregulated European radio market), the ability of the USA to remain economically superior in the transnational entertainment business is in question.

This reduction in economic presence has occurred at the same time as the rapid sequence of events resulting in the music industries' absorption into the more extended and powerful structures of the entertainment business. While the contents and formats of United States media remain influential, it is questionable whether this influence will persist as forcefully as it has in the form of the domination of world markets by Anglo-American popular music. The recent appointment of a Frenchman (Alain Levy) as the international head of Polygram (80 per cent owned by Philips, a corporation which originated in the Netherlands and whose headquarters is there), is perhaps symptomatic of the nature of these changes. Symptomatic also are the spaces which have opened up for smaller music markets (local, regional and national) within the unremittingly powerful yet increasingly distanced umbrella of the transnational entertainment industries. As John Preston, head of British BMG, recently argued, the music industries guarantee cultural diversity. They guarantee it, that is, as far as the ability of locally produced musics to penetrate transnational markets is concerned, and to the extent that local markets can support the production of culturally diverse music. Much local music, then, remains within its own commercial context and remains, also, without aspirations to the transnational. Of significance within these complex shifts and realignments are the rapidly changing music technologies which allow musicians greater determination over the immediate circumstances of music's production, and a greater degree of autonomy in relation to other musicians and the industries.

The first two papers in this special issue address the twin issues of the likely reduction in Anglo-American dominance and the increasing role that has come to be played by technologies in the formation of musicians' consciousness. Simon Frith argues that the formation of Anglo-American music and its dominance of the international market was a specific historical event. Recent developments, both inside and outside the musical industries and musical cultures, have challenged the cultural and economic position of Anglo-American music. Frith suggests that Britain's crucial role – as both talent pool and a test market – is changing under pressure from the multinationalization of the music industry, new technologies and new sources of profits, new geo-political relations, and the redefinition of the place of national identity in the global market.

Paul Théberge approaches the question of recent changes in music technologies from an unusual but insightful standpoint, that of the magazines through which technologies are presented and mediated to musicians. The music press has remained relatively unexamined as a site for the mediation of discursive formations within popular music. As Théberge observes, 'it is quite probable that more critical attention was paid to the rise of MTV during its first two years of operation than to the music press during the past two decades.' Such neglect is surprising, says Théberge, 'given the degree to which all modern industries ... have become dependent upon specialized periodicals to help organize both their internal and external relations' (270). An examination of these periodicals within the rapidly shifting world of music technologies reveals that the 'loaded symbolic terrain' (274) of the relationship of musicians to their instruments is now mediated discursively through these publications to an increasing extent as other recordings and musicians become less relevant to the formation of knowledge, skills and consciousness. Romantic notions of authenticity and personal expression are reconstituted. The nostalgia for old technologies is transformed into the value of new technologies. The new technologies become future, retrospective demarcators of a sense of community constituted and constructed in the present through these very same technologies. 'It is interesting', says Théberge, 'to explore the manner in which the musicians' magazines themselves work to simultaneously construct their readers as both a kind of musical "community" and a market' (283). If modern technologies have facilitated a dislocation and reconstitution of place in relation to space, then, equally, they have facilitated a collapsing and relocation of past and future in the present.

Paul Rutten's paper offers a theorization of relationships between the transnational and the local. Taking as his starting point the situation of Dutch music, Rutten develops a typology in which the positions of countries in relation to processes of transnational production and consumption are located in one of four categories: those of countries with a big phonogram market, a big share of local music in the turnover of that local market, and a relatively important role for local sounds in transnational markets; those of countries with a big phonogram market, a big share of local music in the turnover of that local market, and a relatively unimportant role for local sounds in transnational markets; those of countries with a small phonogram market, a big share of local music in the turnover of that local market, and a relatively unimportant role for local sounds in transnational markets; and those of countries with a small phonogram market, a small share of local music in the turnover of that local market, and a relatively unimportant role for local sounds in transnational markets. Countries in the first position are the USA and the UK. Of particular interest to those attending the conference was the fact that two countries illustrative of the final position are the Netherlands and Canada.

Typologies such as the one developed by Rutten are helpful in thinking through the logic of relationships between the transnational and the local. But as Rutten notes, they can only function as a starting point for research into 'the position of a country and its local music within the force field outlined here (299) in this typology. 'Having determined the specific situation of each country which interests us,' concludes Rutten, 'we must grasp those structural factors which shape the context within which the music industry operates' (301). This is what the papers by Robert Wright and Jody Berland achieve in relation to the position of the conference's host country, Canada.

Canada has been peripheral as a focus of analysis in cultural studies. Further, cultural studies in Canada has not displayed an identity analogous to those which have been constructed, contentiously, around the practice of cultural studies in the UK, the USA and Australia. Both situations can be read as symptomatic of the historical and structural forces which have formed 'Canada'. Berland has elsewhere been eloquent on the consequences of these forces, consequences whose depiction and analysis invite parallels with analyses of gender and power:

> While 'Canada' is defined more than ordinarily as a unity bonded by technology, our media more than ordinarily draw us into exterior landscapes. Situated in many places at the same time, tuned in, hooked up, wired into, we know how to see ourselves as part of a global village and to see its boundarylessness as the essence of who we are. Thus the frequent gender analogies for Canada in relation to the U.S.A.: in contemporary feminist analysis, woman is always Other to a dominant power in relation to whom she gains (momentary) advantage through submission, becoming consequently untidy in establishing clear boundaries to her self. It is a state which is intimately related to resentment and to silence and which tends to be articulated, if at all, in a discourse of absence. Thus Canadian culture, manifested in much spoken and unspoken *ressentiment*, a revenge against the present which preserves its own absence by denying its rage. (Berland, 1988: 347)

It is not difficult to see why the study of English-Canadian culture (and perhaps, even more specifically – given the fragmented, sutured and positioned quality of Canadian cultures – the study of English-Ontario culture) from within English-Canada resonates with concerns and issues germane to the contemporary situations and analyses of transnational and local music industries, and of the relationships between them. It is also not difficult to see how this kind of study resonates more generally with concerns and issues prominent within contemporary cultural studies. As Berland observes at the beginning of her paper, 'in a time when controversies about local, national, and international cultural identities, movements and economies have moved to the forefront of academic discussion, Canada's situation is therefore both exemplary and anomalous.' In Canada, continues Berland, 'the cultural and economic problems accompanying nationalization-denationalization-internationalization of the media have been very visible where they are elsewhere more latent . . . and invisible where elsewhere they are more overt' (315).

It is Wright who details the history and contradictions of policies and cultural protectionism in relation to the Canadian recording industry. In a situation where identities of English-Canadian musical culture were at worst tenuous, fragmented, unformed and unspoken, folded within a double articulation of silence and absence (Shepherd and Giles, 1989), or at best developed and spoken only in complex relation to those of United States musical culture (Wright, 1988), policies such as those of the Sound Development Recording Progam – replacing cultural capital with financial capital – could result only in the orientation of successful Canadian musicians towards the sounds of transnational market-places. Policies of cultural protectionism have hardly helped the development of 'Canadian' culture. If anything they have made it markedly more difficult for distinctive forms of English-Canadian culture to emerge. In this sense the serious attention that Wright gives to William Watson's *National Pastimes: The*

Economics of Canadian Leisure, a work published by the 'conservative, free market-oriented think-tank – the Fraser Institute', is not inappropriate. Watson argues that we should be subsidizing activities that teach Canadians about each other, in which case, observes Wright (308), 'the pertinent criteria for eligibility as Canadian content should therefore be the "Canadianness" of a recording's subject matter rather than of its production.' This line of thought raises the difficult question of the relationship of sounds to the meanings and affective states constructed through them, a theme that bubbled to the surface more than once during the conference.

Berland's paper situates debates concerning Canadian cultural policy and its relationship to music within the context of the increasing transnationalization of music and questions of colonization, nationalism and national identity. Engaging such issues in the Canadian context inevitably raises the spectre of free trade and the question of whether the Free Trade Agreement really does create a 'level playing field' within which Canadians and Americans can compete equally within one market-place, or whether it constitutes the logical conclusion of processes through which the United States media and cultural industries have increasingly colonized Canadian spaces as lucrative yet peripheral markets. Berland details the development of free trade as it relates to Canadian cultural processes and institutions, and the issues and debates that such development has occasioned. She then moves on to narrow the focus to the music industry, observing that within the economic and legal frameworks created by free trade the protectionist policies described and analyzed by Wright (policies, it should be remembered, that are contradictory in terms of their avowed aims of sustaining and encouraging Canadian musical culture) must become 'increasingly fragile both economically and politically' (321). This contradiction and fragility has created an environment in which 'Canadian agents, producers, musicians and owners of independent labels have been angry and disturbed at the difficulty of working within their own national market' (322).

This anger, this desire 'to seek repossession', to 'become autonomous as producers or as consumers of popular music' (322) begs the question of what is to be done, a question that neither Wright nor Berland address. The question of what is to be done is, however, addressed in another context in Sara Cohen's paper on popular music and urban regeneration initiatives in Liverpool. Liverpool is a city which people have been leaving in large numbers as a result of high unemployment. It is a city that musicians have likewise left in order to achieve fame and fortune elsewhere, primarily in London. Financially racked as a consequence of disputes between radical local government and the national policies of Thatcherism, Liverpool has sought to regenerate itself partially by capitalizing on its reputation as a city that has produced such luminaries as The Beatles and Frankie Goes to Hollywood, groups that are themselves resented within Liverpool because of their failure to contribute to the cultural and financial well-being of the area. There thus exists within Liverpool a sense of absence, silence and resentment that is reminiscent, if only superficially, of the situation in English-Canada, together with a sense that out of this silence and absence something good can be built.

The Institute of Popular Music at the University of Liverpool (where Cohen is a Research Fellow) has become involved in a research capacity with a number of projects based on local government's recognition that popular music is not something to be 'treated with disdain by public policy' (which is what many local authorities in the UK have done, focusing instead on the 'high' arts as a potential tourist attraction and source of revenue), but a cultural form that in itself has 'economic and social potential' (331). The participation of the Institute in regeneration programmes, while forward-looking in breaking down the barriers between academic analysis and actual cultural practice, is not without its problems. In a lucid paper rich in detail and information, Cohen highlights the manner in which the practices of the transnational music industries and the policies of central government can have complex, contradictory and frustrating consequences for local situations such as that of Liverpool. Further, the involvement of local government, education and the private sector in initiatives which engage these situations can result in power struggles. Each sector, says Cohen, 'embraces a set of particular discourses whose confrontation often results in misunderstandings or hostility' (338). Yet despite these difficulties, it is clear that the Institute is having an effect, and a positive one, and that there is a great deal to be learnt about the intersection of the academic and the practical from its activities.

If Cohen's paper is symptomatic of a gaze towards the future, then so also is Laurie Brown's. Brown's paper is the only contribution in these proceedings from a non-academic, from someone whose experiences of the music industry are from the inside (Laurie Brown was, until recently, a video jockey and producer with City TV's MuchMusic, the Toronto based, English-language equivalent of the USA's MTV). Brown's paper is uncompromising in establishing, as Berland has, that 'the Big Question facing Canadian artists is not "Who am I?" ... but, rather, "Where is Here?"' (345), and that 'Here' is essentially 'not "There"' (354). It is uncompromising in establishing, as Berland has, that Canada is 'a different country with different experiences, tastes and sounds, not to mention economic institutions and ideologies' (322). But while Berland questions, correctly, 'whether Canadian culture can be identified or defended as a unitary "national subject"' (322), Brown seeks to identify from this difference of absences and silences a distinctively English-Canadian musical presence. What Brown identifies is not so much a static style easily equatable with specific social groups, but a complex trajectory – country, folk, urban and significantly female – that speaks in an ironic and sometimes underground fashion to being here and not there. It could be argued that what Brown is articulating is a desire more than a reality. But such criticism, in the English-Canadian context, requires careful and sensitive handling. Firstly, even if many successful English-Canadian musicians do sound eminently 'mainstream', indistinguishable from the transnational norm, it does not follow that the English-Canadian experience of these or other non-Canadian artists is identical, or even similar, to the parallel experience south of the border. As has been argued elsewhere:

> The condition of created dependency, of invaded space and transgressed boundaries, is not identical, even in the lived experience of the 'popular mind', with a condition manifesting cultural self-sufficiency and self-confidence. The logic of the English-Canadian experience can bear a different set of relationships to mass mediated transnational musics, even when produced by Canadians, than the experiences of those born and raised in the United States can. (Shepherd and Giles, 1989: 122)

Secondly and more importantly, desire itself, and particularly the desire of repossession and autonomy, does not lie outside of discourse. If, in the words of Wright's assessment of the impact of 'Tears Are Not Enough' (the David Foster tune, originally intended for use as a love theme in a United States film, which became the Canadian equivalent of 'We Are the World'), 'Canadians rallied around a mythic nationalism, a sentiment of such power that it could, even in the 1980s, suspend reason' (Wright, 1988: 40), then it is the sentiment that has to be understood as part of a socially constructed reality. In this sense, it is possible to comment that:

> The point is neither that Canadian nationalism is mythic, nor that it suspends reason. The point is that the myth – if it is myth – has the power to suspend reason. It is this power, this desire to possess and be possessed by a national identity as evoked and articulated through the contradictory and paradoxical dynamics of English-Canadian musical life that needs to be investigated. (Shepherd and Giles, 1989: 116)

Brown is optimistic as she wrestles with this challenge. She sees paradoxical opportunities for English-Canadian music as a result of free trade, and concludes that 'a maturing regional voice' (354) will emerge to give expression to 'Canadianicity'.

Brown's paper inevitably raises the question of the relationship between sounds and the meanings and affects constructed through them. If a sound is distinctively Canadian, then how does 'Canadianicity' get into the sound? This question lingered menacingly throughout the conference in the presentations of Théberge, Wright, Berland and Cohen (who is researching the 'Liverpool sound'). It is a question tackled head on by Lawrence Grossberg. Grossberg's paper is concerned primarily with perceived changes in rock's politics. 'Most discussions of the politics of contemporary rock', he argues, 'start by assuming that, in some sense, rock has lost its political edge.' This being the case, continues Grossberg, 'it does seem odd that there is so much energy being directed against it' (356). Grossberg concludes that the political edge of rock has come, historically, not so much from inside rock, as from the opposition mounted against it. This opposition occurred (at least initially), not so much because rock entered into 'any explicit ideological struggle or political resistance' (357), but because it sought to counter the quietism or conservatism implicit in the social and economic climate of the post-war United States. The rock music of this era was about a rewriting of the mainstream, and paradoxically so. In challenging quietism and conservatism, it none the less accommodated itself to the optimism, consumerism and liberalism that characterized the period. Rock was essentially about culture and fun. Rock, claims Grossberg, 'sought to open culture to the needs and experiences of its own audiences, not to deny or overturn the consensual and institutional structures which had made those experiences, and rock's existence, possible' (359).

If rock is about everyday life – 'a relation that makes it particularly important in everyday life' – and if, indeed, it is a form of music – 'while this is quite obvious, discussions of rock often miss the unique relation of music and power' (360) – then there is a need to theorize the relationship of music to everyday life. Grossberg explores the notion that music is 'the most powerful affective agency in human life' (361) in its capacity to transcend the everyday. 'Everyday life is itself organized by the rhythms of places and spaces, and by specific configurations of places.' This is merely to say continues Grossberg, 'that music, or more specifically rock, organizes the mattering maps by which everyday life becomes navigable and hence, liveable' (362).

The special ability of music to do this depends, however, on a contradictory 'deterritorializing', the power to destroy 'the codes which guarantee the repeatability necessary to both power and everyday life' (362). There seems to be a certain transcendence being claimed here as a result of the ability of music to both territorialize and deterritorialize, to articulate 'place in the service of space, stability in the service of mobility' (362). If music is, indeed, about 'disciplined mobilization', then the directions indicated in Grossberg's paper require further exploration and theorization. It remains unclear, for example, whether the special status and ability being claimed here for music depends on the more traditional argument that it is in certain respects pre-linguistic, pre-symbolic and pre-Oedipal, in a certain sense capable of deterritorializing socially structured locations because it begins life outside them. There is a danger in this line of argument that has been identified by Richard Middleton in respect of the contributions of French poststructuralist thought to an understanding of music's affective power, its sociality. Middleton's criticisms are directed at the later work of Barthes. Like other French poststructuralists, says Middleton,

> who wanted to ground discourse on extralinguistic forces and dispositions, the later Barthes is open to the suspicion that 'anything goes': that along with meaning, the category of critique is abandoned, leaving the field open to political quietism, untheorized spontaneism, or apolitical hedonism. This danger may be attributed precisely to the relative neglect of historically positioned structures of meaning. (Middleton, 1990: 266–7)

Grossberg's arguments are nothing if not grounded. This grounding, then, points to the need to theorize music's capacity to structure, position and locate, and its capacity to at the same time transcend the everyday, in a way which distances itself from this tendency in poststructuralist thought. A way forward might be to problematize the notions of 'music' and 'noise' in terms of which Grossberg's arguments are couched. Since the polysemic meanings of the term 'music' are discursively constituted, and since, as a consequence, its taken-for-granted use may, indeed, indicate that we do not really know what we are talking about when we use it, it might be more fruitful to concentrate on the physical and in a certain sense 'given' phenomenon of sound as in some way constitutive of 'music', and on the range of signifying potentials it manifests. The work of Peter Wicke (1989; see also Wicke, 1990) has already moved in this direction by theorizing the sound of music, not as providing the material ground for the constitution of signifiers, but as a social medium that is both structured and structuring. As a socially structured mobile matrix that is both fluid and tangible, the sound of music is implicated in the construction of the meanings and affective states it mediates, but not deterministically so. It transcends the specific locations of visual space, but is grounded, ultimately, in the human body and the sonic-spatial relationships the configured and configuring body has with the world surrounding and touching it (Shepherd and Wicke, forthcoming, 1992).

Grossberg's paper is valuable in bringing to the fore and focusing an issue (the articulation of constructed meanings and affects through the materials of music) that is crucial to the understanding of all dimensions of musical practice. It is perhaps not coincidental that this issue should have been present in so many of the papers at a conference whose primary concern was, after all, the institutional and policy dimensions of musical practice. The presence of this underlying theme is salutary. The institutional and policy dimensions of music are studied, presumably, because there is an interest in music, in the meanings and affective states in whose construction music is, in one way or another, implicated.

It is none the less important to accept that our understanding of the processes through which music is involved in these constructions is at best limited. That the processes through which music is involved in the construction and mediation of meaning, affect and relevancy are complex is illustrated graphically in the final paper of this collection by Will Straw. However, if Straw's paper speaks to the intersection of the institutional and the affective, it speaks also to the intersection of the transnational and the local which emerged as the conference's principal theme. Straw draws a distinction between the 'older notion' of a musical community – which 'presumes a particular population group whose composition is relatively stable . . . and whose involvement in music takes the form of an ongoing exploration of a particular musical idiom said to be rooted organically in a geographically specific historical heritage' – and that of a musical scene – 'that cultural space within which a range of musical practices coexist, interacting with each other within a variety of processes of differentiation and according to widely varying trajectories of change and cross-fertilization' (371).

There is every reason to see why the notion of a 'scene' is appropriate to attempts to grasp musical localities in Canada. These localities are characterized by the intermingling of diverse cultures which in their displacement manoeuvre on a terrain of various positionalities mediated externally. But the notion of a 'scene' is equally if not more important to grasping the wider conditions of rock's 'decline and death', the loss of its political edge (a topic already examined critically by Grossberg in this issue), its replacement as a preoccupation for youth by dance-based pop music and heavy metal. The aura of alternative rock's teleology, its constitution as political difference leading to political change, had been superseded by the shifting sands of the local, sands which themselves are symptomatic of the role played by the musical differentiation within the international culture of popular music. Straw's paper examines these trends by reference to recent trajectories in dance music and alternative rock. Within the latter, argues Straw, 'the relationship of different local or regional scenes to each other is no longer one in which specific communities emerge to enact a forward movement to which others are drawn.' Rather, he concludes, '[e]ach local space has evolved, to varying degrees, the range of musical vernaculars emergent within others.' (376) Thus, in Canada, for example, musical scenes come to be constituted partially through practices and readings located elsewhere. The local can only be local in specific and concrete relations to transnational practices, a point established earlier in this issue by Rutten. 'Basing a politics of local or Canadian music on the search for musical forms whose relationship to musical communities is that of a long-term and evolving expressivity', says Straw, 'will lead us [. . .] to overlook ways in which the making and remaking of alliances between communities are the crucial political processes within popular music' (368).

Straw's paper graciously leaves the door open for the possibility that the 'older notion' of a musical community may be appropriate to the examination of musical practices of other times and places. But there remains none the less a hint of critique. 'Those encountering ethnomusicological studies for the first time after an apprenticeship in the hermeneutics of suspicion may', observes Straw, 'be struck by the prominence within them of notions of cultural totality or claims concerning the expressive unity of musical practices' (367). If the raising of complex questions of affect at this conference was salutary, then it was important also in engaging a set of problematics experienced far more forcefully and urgently within progressive developments in musicology and ethnomusicology and in more musicologically oriented approaches to critical popular-music studies. The satisfaction of the conference for me lay in a sense that a set of problematics was finally emerging which subsumed the concerns both of critically minded musicologists and ethnomusicologists, and of musically interested cultural theorists.

I would like to thank Janice Yalden (Dean of Arts at Carleton University) and Marilyn Marshall (Dean of Social Sciences) for the financial support to the Centre which made the conference possible. I would like to thank also my colleagues in the Centre (particularly the sessional lecturers and students) without whose labour the conference could not have happened. But my greatest debt is to Wiz Long, the Administrative Assistant in Carleton's Department of Music, whose expertise and dedication ensured the conference's success.

References

Berland, Jody (1988) 'Locating listening: technological space, popular music, Canadian mediation', *Cultural Studies*, 2: 343–58.

Middleton, Richard (1990) *Studying Popular Music*. Milton Keynes: Open University Press.

Shepherd, John (1990) editor, *Alternative Musicologies/Les Musicologies Alternatives*, special issue of the *Canadian University Music Review*, 10 (2): 137–56.

Shepherd, John and Giles, Jennifer (1989) 'The politics of silence: problematics for the analysis of English-Canadian musical culture', *Australian/Canadian Studies*, 7 (1–2) 113–25.

Shepherd, John and Wicke, Peter (forthcoming, 1992) *The Sound of Music: Meaning and Power in Culture*. Cambridge: Polity Press.

Wicke, Peter (1989) 'Rockmusik – Aspekte einer Faszination', *Weimare Beitrage* 27: 98–126.

Wicke, Peter (1990) 'Rock music: dimensions of a mass medium – meaning production through popular music', in Shepherd (1990).

Wright, Robert (1988) '"Dream, comfort, memory, despair": Canadian popular musicians and the dilemma of nationalism, 1968–1972', *Journal of Canadian Studies*, 22 (4) 27–43.

John Shepherd is Professor of Music and Director of the School for Studies in Art and Culture at Carleton University

ARTICLES

SIMON FRITH

ANGLO-AMERICA AND ITS DISCONTENTS

I

I started writing this paper during the early stages of the fight for the leadership of the Conservative Party which led so unexpectedly to the demise of Margaret Thatcher. What was already clear was that the Tories were split on attitudes to Europe and that these, in turn, reflected attitudes to the USA. To put it crudely, the pro-Europeans, like Michael Heseltine, were implicitly anti-American, while those who believed in 'the special relationship', like Mrs Thatcher, were explicitly anti-European.

This is not the place to explore these arguments further (or the way they were complicated by the Gulf War), but they did reflect a broader British anxiety. Is our identity essentially linguistic, reaching across the Atlantic to North America and the Caribbean, south to the old colonies, to Australia, South Africa, to India and Hong Kong? Or are we all Europeans now, part of a free market that is set to expand East, our Island status finally sacrificed to the Channel Tunnel?

From a pop fan's perspective this question may seem silly. Contemporary popular music, rock, *is* Anglo-American; the language of success is English. And, whatever I may say, musicians in France and Japan, Brazil and the Philippines, Finland and Zaire know where musical power lies. Even so, as an Anglo, I'm not convinced that the Anglo-American domination of worldwide popular music is as extensive or secure as it seems.

To begin with, 'Anglo-American' music is a relatively recent invention, dating from 1963–4 and the rise of The Beatles. Before then Britain was just as insignificant and derivative a nation in pop terms as any other European country. Our Elvis Presley, Cliff Richard, was no more important outside

Britain (and the Commonwealth) than France's Elvis Presley, Johnny Halliday, was outside France (and the French colonies) or than Italy's Elvis Presley, Little Tony, outside Italy. Young British listeners then were dependent for rock and roll sounds on Radio Luxembourg, and the British music industry agitated volubly for protectionist measures: guaranteed airplay for British records and British songs; exclusion of touring American musicians to protect the livelihood of the locals. In tracing the global progress of 'Rock Around the Clock', say, or the Twist, we would find no particular reason for singling out their British impact. My first question, then, is, if there was a time *before* Anglo-American pop, couldn't there also be a time after it?

The peculiarity of the post-Beatles situation is also indicated by a brief look at other media. International book publishing could be characterized, analogously, as Anglo-American; international magazine publishing could not – publishing giants from Spain and Germany dominate both continental Europe and sectors of the British market. The global market for films and television programmes is American rather than Anglo-American; British film policy has long been organized, unsuccessfully, around the defence of the British film industry; the export of British television remains largely restricted to 'quality' shows. Even more strikingly, the world's most played and watched game, Association football, has little appeal in the USA, while its national sports, American football and baseball, are not much watched anywhere else.

In short, Anglo-Americanism isn't an inevitable description of mass global culture, even in those media in which a shared language is at a premium. The USA dominates the worldwide film and television industries because of its market size and the economies of scale: its producers can cover their production costs domestically and undercut any other producers internationally. And its market dominance has enabled it to exercise cultural dominance too – not simply in the spoken language on the screen, but in visual and narrative terms too. What has come to be seen as film and television entertainment – in terms of genre and spectacle and pace – was defined by Hollywood studio conventions and American cinemagoers' tastes. Why didn't this happen in music too?

Within the industry itself, two reasons are usually given for Britain's importance in international music-making: first, the UK is a *talent pool*; second, it is a *test market*. My second question is whether either of these situations is permanent.

Britain became a pop talent pool in the 1960s and 1970s for a variety of local reasons to do with the peculiar characteristics of its musicians in terms of youth culture and education, but also because of our long familiarity with American song forms and song language (though there was nothing inevitable about this – Britain has not produced more jazz musicians than other European countries, for example). By the 1980s though, just as convincing 'American' musicians were emerging from Sweden and Australia, from Germany and Iceland, and the rise of 'world music' is a reminder that these days successful Western pop can come from anywhere –

in this case mostly via Paris. Britain's uniqueness as a pop talent pool can no longer be taken for granted.

Its importance as a test market is, equally, a matter of structural, historical circumstances (a national monopoly broadcasting service, an influential music press, a music culture more marked by stylistic differences than by class or geographical mobility). British pop norms were thus important when the international business thought in terms of youth and fashion (and British singles sales were accurate indicators of future worldwide album sales and stardom); they are less so for the pursuit of the yuppie demographic and the corporate tie-in. Since punk, British taste has, in fact, been decidedly erratic in international terms (the 'second British invasion' of the USA, in the early days of MTV, simply reflected a brief moment of revived teen marketing). These days record companies are as likely to use the 'grown-up' Dutch market as the British youth market as their testing ground.

The irony of this situation is that it was Britain's rise to importance as talent pool and test market that changed the conditions of musical production and consumption that gave it that importance in the first place. The immediate business effect of Britain's American impact in the mid-sixties was the invasion of London by American A&R and marketing teams; by the end of the decade Britain's leading musical 'exports' were being sold by non-British companies. Twenty years on, EMI remains Britain's only major label, and the seventies rock independents, like Island, have been absorbed by foreign companies (even Virgin Records is now dependent on Japanese investment).

In the music business, then, 'Anglo-American' describes a particular historical period and conceals a greater dependence of the Anglo on the American than the order of the terms might suggest. At the same time, the usual snootiness about European rock conceals a much longer history in which British musicians have been part of a European (rather than American) music world. The Beatles, after all, survived as a group (and forged the style that made them famous) playing clubs in Germany, and all 'alternative' British musicians since, from the progressive rockers like Soft Machine and Henry Cow at the end of the 1960s to the punk and indie bands of the 1970s and 1980s have been dependent for their bedrock income on European clubs, European broadcasters, European festivals, and European audiences. The history of British club music has, similarly, from the 'discotheques' of the 1960s to 1980s Hi-NRG, Balearic beat and acid house, been the history of a European phenomenon, even if one dependent for its sounds on Black American musicians.

There are obvious economic reasons why, for a young band or little label, Europe is a better market than the USA: it is nearer, more compact, and more familiar in its promotional institutions. Even such an obviously Anglo-American form as heavy metal, for example, now has a European identity (to which British bands must subscribe) – a touring circuit, radio and TV shows, a German-based magazine (with English and Spanish editions), a pool of musicians who all sound the same whether they're from Germany or Sweden, Britain or, now, Eastern Europe. As it becomes harder for *any* group or record company to cover production and promotion costs on British sales alone, so it becomes necessary for *all* British bands to go for international sales from the start, and Europe is not only nearer than the USA, these days it also generates more music income. The 1980s deregulation of European broadcasting, for instance, led to a huge rise in the demand for music programming, whether in the form of videos, studio appearances or concert footage, and late eighties pop groups like the Pet Shop Boys or Bananarama planned their marketing strategy accordingly.

What we have here is less a new invasion of Europe by British pop than the development of European pop institutions (commercial music TV and radio, teen magazines) to go alongside the well-established European rock institutions. British musicians and entrepreneurs are key players in these institutions but they are not British institutions. Thus Britain's most significant radio deejay, John Peel (who began his career in the 1960s as a British voice in Texas) is now effectively a Euro deejay. He broadcasts weekly for both Finnish radio and Hilversum, and his BBC World Service show is probably now more important promotionally than his Radio 1 programmes. These days he includes more European than American sounds in his playlist.

From this perspective, 1992 (the year the European Community becomes a free-trade area, taking down the final barriers to the flow of goods, services and labour, harmonizing the various national laws on licensing and copyright) marks the logical end of a process, rather than a beginning. Production is already centralized in pan-European terms – most 'British' records, tapes and CDs and all British record sleeves are now manufactured in France or Germany. As for taste (using the charts for a moment as its basic measure), British consumers already have more in common with their European neighbours than with the USA, at least in terms of new music. 'Anglo-American', one might conclude, is just another name for 'classic' rock.

II

What are the implications of this for national and international pop?

The first thing we need to do is rethink what is meant by a 'major' record company. In the last decade there have been two significant changes in the international music business: first, the USA is no longer economically dominant – RCA's absorption into the German publishing company, BMG (the Bertelsmann Group), and Sony's takeover of CBS, leaves WEA (now Time-Warner) as the only American 'giant' (the others are both European – Britain's Thorn EMI, and the Dutch Polygram); second, this takeover activity (also reflected in internal restructurings and lower-level deals like the Mitsushita purchase of MCA) marks a recomposition of the hardware/software relationship. As both the pace of technological change and the consumer boom in domestic electronic goods slow down, so ownership of the software (the films and music) becomes more desirable. The digital-recording age has reached the stage the electrical-recording age reached in the 1960s.

Two points follow from this, one conceptual, one methodological. Conceptually we can no longer sensibly define the international music market in nationalistic terms, with some countries (the USA, the UK) imposing their culture on others. This does not describe the cultural consequences of the new multinationals: whose culture do Sony-CBS and BMG-RCA represent?

Methodologically, we can no longer measure the multinational penetration of national cultures with statistics of personal consumption. (How many records sold in each country? On which labels? With which artists?) The basic unreliability of these figures, particularly in smaller (and/or pirate-ridden) markets distorts the picture in the majors' favour (their sales are more likely to be reported) and, anyway, as their income base shifts from primary to secondary rights ownership, so record sales cease to be the best measure of even their success.

Measuring national music success is equally problematic, and a simple reference to record labels is certainly inadequate. One effect of the digital 'revolution' in recording (another aspect of the changing relationship between hard and software) has been to transform the grounds of 'local' production: what Paul Théberge has characterized as a 'universalization' of sound' means that music can sound the same (share the global acoustic) wherever it comes from; what once were 'demos' are now to all intents and purposes 'finished' products. The competition for 'access' to the international market therefore now depends less on live performance than on initial studio work, and 'national' production companies are more and more likely to license their products territory by territory than in a blanket major deal. Analysis of national sales, label by label, doesn't tell us much about either where the music comes from or where the money goes.

In short, the standard analytic model of multinationals versus local 'national' producers is no longer helpful. In the new leisure world, global leisure corporations control the publication, transmission, distribution and licensing of goods (books, films, programmes, songs, stars and stories) which are produced by local producers using local facilities (musicians, engineers, designers, writers, etc.).

The risk of producing a market failure is thus also borne locally. The majors no longer record in their own studies, using their own producers; but, rather, rely on independent producers and 'little labels' to do their research and development for them, and employ a myriad of independent promotion teams and pluggers and impresarios to orchestrate any success. The pattern here is much like that in the film industry, and as the overall costs of music marketing shift (promotion costs are now greater than production costs), so, in turn, there is an increasing emphasis on pre-selling, on multimedia exploitation, on blockbusters and superstars.

In this model, the majors don't share some supranational identity, something to be *imposed* culturally around the globe, but, rather, control an information network, so that whatever sells in one country can be mass-marketed in another. The spread of majors' offices around the world, then, is designed less to make more efficient the local selling of international talent.

Robert Burnett has divided the history of Swedish rock into three eras: the production of local versions of Anglo-American sounds for local consumption in the 1960s and 1970s; the production of local sounds for local consumption in the 1970s and 1980s (an effect of punk nationalism and the search for a specifically Swedish rock – articulated most often linguistically, by songs sung in Swedish); the production of local sounds for the international market in the 1980s and 1990s, as people began to realize that in today's world what matters is not just that all music from all sources should sound approximately the same, but that such sameness should also make a difference. Milli Vanilli, Roxette and Sinead O'Connor represent three versions of the same process: 'local' music made with a global perspective (and what seems old-fashioned is the British belief, exemplified in the Stone Roses, that local cult success alone should guarantee access to the American market).

III

Which brings me back to my starting question. What is Anglo-American music now? What does 'national' popular music mean?

What I have been describing as 'global music' stands in a kind of commercial/folk dialectic with 'world music' – the former is the sound to which the latter is a response, whether aurally or ideologically. And 'global culture' does not mean American culture (those cultural artefacts that best express American values are, for that reason, those least likely to become global successes, although there is 'American' global music – Madonna, say – just as there is British and Swedish and Bolivian global music). The cultural imperialist model – nation versus nation – must be replaced by a postimperial model of an infinite number of local experiences of (and responses to) something globally shared.

In this context the 'local' is defined by reference not to a specific geography or community but, rather, to a shared sense of place that is, itself, part of the global picture. In such a mapping process, one's sense of musical locality depends both on the immediate material circumstances (venues, audiences, etc.) and also on 'reference' groups, on identities and fantasies that are themselves mediated globally. 'Locality' is produced as our sense of difference from the global – it is not a spontaneous expression of given, hard-held local traditions.

The question becomes whether 'America' can continue to be the mythical locale of popular culture as it has been through most of this century. As I've suggested, there are reasons now to suppose that 'America' itself, as a pop cultural myth, no longer bears much relationship to the USA as a real place *even in the myth* – that is, to be American no longer means either moving there or sharing its consumer tastes. It's not just that America is no longer the dominant media market in statistical terms, but also that its very cultural forms are now everywhere available: to sing in English no longer means to sing in English; it just means to be a pop star, so that, for example, the global impact of rap has not been worldwide sales of US rap acts, but numerous local, English-language adaptations – there are Dutch rap acts and South African rap acts and Filipino rap acts and Hawaiian rap acts (any of whom has as much chance to make it globally as the rappers from the Bronx or LA).

Where this leaves the Anglo I'm not yet sure, although there are reasons to suspect that 'Europe' *is* becoming a new mythical space, with rhythms of memory and identity, war and migration, colonialism and return, which are decidedly un-American. To put this another way, the end of the Cold War means not just the end of the Soviet Union as an object of fantasy (whether as good or evil) but also of the USA. As Lyotard put it in another context, we have no grand models now. In pop terms this means that our concerns have become more localized (mapped onto the body and the dance floor, onto the pay check and the sales slip) just as what we listen to goes global; in personal terms it means that I identify now with the Euro-pop of the Pet Shop Boys (wry, civilized, with a sincerity beyond irony) rather than with the old, bombastic, ambitious Anglo-American sound of U2. We – Anglos, Europeans – no longer want the world; we just want to enjoy it.

PAUL THÉBERGE

MUSICIANS' MAGAZINES IN THE 1980S: THE CREATION OF A COMMUNITY AND A CONSUMER MARKET

Introduction

We live today, or so we are told, in an electronic culture – a culture dominated by the audio/visual environments of radio and television broadcasting and instantaneous data transmission via computer, telephone and satellite. This is, of course, true; nevertheless, whenever I enter the local newsstand I am still struck by the enormous number of newspapers and magazines on offer, everything from mass-circulation tabloids and gossip magazines to far more limited-circulation periodicals devoted to the most obscure special-interest groups. Indeed, it is perhaps ironic that instead of diminishing the number of available publications, electronic culture appears to be contributing its own considerable weight to the shelves of most newsstands: witness the number of glossy monthlies devoted to computers, CDs and audio-video equipment. Print culture is dead! Long live print culture!

A similar dynamic appears to exist in the world of popular music: during the 1960s, 1970s and 1980s, successive waves of new technology have transformed the manner in which music is produced, distributed and consumed. Not surprisingly, perhaps, one of the most striking aspects of this development has been the number of new magazines that have appeared on newsstands to support the burgeoning market for these new technologies. Nowhere is this phenomenon more evident than in the newest group of magazines designed for pop music's vanguard in high-tech musical instruments and recording devices – the popular musicians themselves. Even the titles of this recent crop of music periodicals – *Music Technology*, *Electronic Musician*, *Home & Studio Recording* and *Music, Computers & Software* – trumpet their commitment to new technology and to music production in the brave new world of the so-called 'Electronic Cottage'.

Of course, there is an easy explanation for all of this: despite heavy competition from the electronic media, magazines remain one of the most economical means for advertisers to reach a specific market for their products (electronic or otherwise) and this is especially true for the musicians' market which is relatively small, highly specialized, and widely dispersed. But, while I would certainly not deny that these magazines are, for the most part, advertiser-driven (indeed, this fact is a central element of much of what follows in this paper), it seems to me that the construction of a consumer market for new musical technology throughout the 1970s and 1980s has been extremely complex, and perhaps unique in many ways. To regard these magazines as simply a function of the promotional apparatus of the musical instrument industry would be to ignore a variety of historical, economic, technical, ideological, social and cultural mediations that have been characteristic of these developments. Not least among these mediations, as I will attempt to argue, has been the manner in which these magazines contribute to a sense of 'community' among musicians in the increasingly internationalized and technical context of contemporary music production.

The role of magazines in musical culture has been largely ignored by historians of the publishing industry and by writers on popular music alike. Theodore Peterson, in his in-depth study of the rise of modern magazine publishing in the twentieth century (1964), makes only passing reference to music periodicals in his chapter on special-interest magazines of the 1950s and early 1960s, before turning his attention to magazines devoted to sports, science, and other interests. Ford's study of specialized publications (1969) lists a number of music and hi-fi magazines in a chapter on leisure periodicals but offers little commentary; and Taft (1982), who contributes a somewhat more varied and updated list, goes no further than to add a one-page discussion of *Rolling Stone*.

In the literature on popular music there is also little serious consideration of the music press (although, as Sarah Thornton has pointed out, a number of pop histories have used the music and trade magazines as a substructure for their own commentaries, adopting and naturalizing their frames of reference in the process; 1990: 88–9). In Chambers' (1985) account of the history of post-war music there are many references to the music press, but little effort is made towards understanding its role in the pop process; Frith (1981) and Chapple and Garofalo (1977) grant the music press a more important place in their studies of popular music but still only devote a few pages each to their discussions of it. Perhaps only in Laing's (1985) discursive analysis of punk rock is there anything approaching a serious assessment of the press as a central element in the 'framing' of popular musical forms. And while there have been numerous biographies of rock groups, such as The Rolling Stones (and many bands of lesser significance as well), the magazine *Rolling Stone* – which has probably sold more copies than the Stones have albums[1] and has had at least as much influence both in and outside the world of music – has received such undivided attention on only two occasions: firstly, in an early series of articles by former staff member Chet Flippo (1974); and secondly, in a recently published book by Robert Draper, *Rolling Stone Magazine: The Uncensored History* (1990), the title of which gives a strong indication of its tendency towards biographical exposé. Indeed, it is quite probable that more critical attention was paid to the rise of MTV during its first two years of operation than to the music press during the past two decades.

Such neglect is surprising, given the degree to which all modern industries (especially the technical and electronics industries of which various music industries are a part) have become dependent upon specialized periodicals to help organize both their internal and external relations (see Ford, 1969: 113–15, and Taft, 1982: 85–7). With respect to music, if everyday language can be considered not as an external adjunct but as a central part of the process by which we 'metaphorically locate, categorize, associate, reflect on, or evaluate music experience' (Feld, 1984: 16), then the press should be regarded as an important focal point in relation to which the production of musical meaning can be studied as a concrete social activity.

Music periodicals are as varied as the many activities that constitute the world of contemporary music-making: the *Standard Periodical Directory* lists several hundred music periodicals published in the United States and Canada, ranging from amateur music society newsletters to industry trade magazines and tip sheets, fanzines, specialized magazines for almost every instrument and musical style imaginable, technical journals for sound engineers and producers, hi-fi magazines, and academic journals. A number of these date from the late nineteenth century and are among the oldest continuously publishing commercial magazines in North America.

In this paper I would like to present an overview of some of the factors that have contributed to the rise of a group of new, highly technical, consumer-oriented musicians' magazines in the field of popular music. I would also like to outline a number of characteristics of these magazines that are perhaps quite unique and to discuss, in a critical way, their implications for their popular-musician readers. The analysis presented here is only part of a much larger research project into the digital and electronic musical instrument industry in the 1980s and its relationship to contemporary musical practice. Because of space/time constraints and the as-yet incomplete nature of this research, much of the following is preliminary, and will, no doubt, be subject to revision as more detailed research continues. Some of the information for this paper was obtained through personal interviews with individuals in the music-instrument and music-publishing industries, and a number of these individuals are listed at the end of the paper as sources even though few are directly quoted in the text.

The context

The context in which the recent proliferation of musicians' magazines has taken place is extremely complex and includes a number of economic, technical and social/historical factors that, although present throughout the post-war period, have become increasingly significant since the late 1970s and early 1980s. Furthermore, these factors are not confined to any one industrial field but relate to a variety of changes occurring more or less simultaneously in the publishing, electronics and music industries.

Firstly, within the world of magazine publishing itself, both the number and circulation of business and special-interest magazines in all fields have increased. Peterson has noted that, while special-interest magazines have been in existence at least since the turn of the century, advances in education, income and leisure time during the 1950s and early 1960s led to a proliferation of new magazines of specialized appeal (1964: 363). Taft claims that this phenomenon has become increasingly important since the mid-1970s and that, while the idea of specialized publications is not itself new, the *degree* of specialization is (1982: 23). The trend in the magazine industry has apparently been one away from the earlier battle with television for mass-market advertising dollars towards a reliance on more specific advertising markets – 'moving to a state of "specialization within specialization" as the market becomes dissected into more minute elements' (Taft, 1982: 17). The contemporary musicians' magazine is one such 'specialization within a specialization' (278).

Evidence of this general trend may be found in recent data published by Statistics Canada (Ifedi, 1990): during the mid-1980s, circulation figures for special-interest magazines in Canada grew by 67 per cent while those of general-interest periodicals declined by 3 per cent. Beyond circulation figures, Statistics Canada reveals a more compelling economic reason for the recent success of this category of periodicals: because they rely more heavily on advertising, special-interest periodicals (especially those containing business content and consumer information) are more profitable publishing enterprises than general-interest magazines (with profits averaging as high as 9 per cent of total revenue compared to 5 per cent average profits in the general-interest area).

One of the largest areas of growth in the special-interest category has been in business periodicals – trade magazines, professional and technical magazines with controlled circulation (such as those directed to sound engineers, record producers or club DJs), etc. – and, while my main interest here is in consumer magazines, it is perhaps worthwhile mentioning these publications, if only briefly. (In the music periodical industry, the business and consumer areas are, in any case, often linked through ownership and editorial control and I will be discussing the significance of this phenomenon below.) Industry has only recently realized the value of 'business-to-business' advertising: studies conducted during the mid-1980s showed that advertising could be more cost effective when directed towards dealers, retailers and other professionals, as well as to end users (see Dougherty, 1986) and this has led some manufacturers to adopt a more integrated approach to advertising and promotion. Such an approach is often encouraged by publishers: for example, Norris Publications, publishers of *Canadian Music Trade* (a musical instrument retailer magazine) and the consumer-oriented *Canadian Musician*, has for several years offered advertisers discounts when they place ads simultaneously in both magazines. The same studies revealed the success rates of various marketing strategies, such as the use of reader-service cards placed in business magazines, and it is interesting to note that service cards of this kind have now become a regular feature of a variety of consumer electronics publications as well, including magazines for musicians, hi-fi enthusiasts and computer users. Publishers of business periodicals also offer other services to industry: some are part of larger communications companies directly engaged in the mounting of trade and consumer shows, and other events, while others publish annual industry directories, an increasingly important function in the fast-changing world of clubs, performance venues, recording studios and video production.

Secondly, technological innovations – in the form of computers, in-house typesetting, data transmission and other work – may have contributed to the increased viability of small-circulation specialized publishing during the 1980s (see Taft, 1982: 342–3). While such technical changes are certainly not as dramatic as the improvements in printing that gave rise to the mass-circulation magazine industry of the late nineteenth century, they have nevertheless become an important aid in overcoming the economic pressures of publishing. In this regard, it is interesting to note that as the more successful musicians' magazines of the 1980s have been absorbed by larger publishing interests, they have also introduced new state-of-the-art desktop production systems and have been expected to share personnel and data banks with other group publications, thus reducing production costs and the size of their support staff. The magazines devoted to hi-tech music-making also maintain contact with industry professionals, contributors and their more up-scale readership through a specialized music-industry computer network called PAN (Performing Artists Network).

A third factor, contributing more directly to the recent increase in the number of musicians' magazines, is related both to the promotional needs of industry and to changing modes of musical production. Since the growth of advertising in the early part of this century, magazine publishing has become part of the marketing system within contemporary capitalism (Peterson, 1964: 18) and, to state the obvious, professional, semiprofessional and amateur musicians are one of the primary markets for musical instrument manufacturers (other markets include the home market – often referred to as the 'consumer' market – and the educational market, among others). According to H. Stith Bennett, this fact has become even more salient since the rise of rock and other forms of popular music based around electronic instruments and sound recording: 'Performers struggled against the disparity between their recorded sound and their live sound throughout the 1950s and 1960s, and slowly their frustrations were turned into a market by musical instrument manufacturers' (1983: 231). This factor has become increasingly significant with the use of samplers, sequencers and special-effects devices of all kinds in studio and stage production during the 1980s.

In this regard, advertising in musicians' magazines is just one among a number of strategies employed by the electronic instrument and sound reinforcement industry in order to reach this critical market: instrument manufacturers often sponsor artists, and, in return, their products are mentioned in tour brochures and album jackets (for example, the album liner notes for a record by Suzanne Vega reveal, in minute detail, not only the brand of guitar, sampler, and other instruments that she and her band use but also the brand of microphone, cymbals, and even her guitar strings). In the 1980s, music video has also been an asset to musical instrument promotion: as one industry spokesperson noted, with music video one can actually see, up close, the make and model of instruments that star performers play – something that is seldom possible in club and stadium concert. Increasingly then, we learn not only *who* plays but also *what* they play as well.

Magazines still form the most direct link between instrument manufacturers and their market, however, and it is interesting to note that while musicians' magazines such as *Down Beat* have existed for many years, it was not until the early 1970s that the emphasis on musicians' 'gear' came to the fore, most notably in magazines such as *Guitar Player*, that have a large, youthful, pop/rock readership. This emphasis has increased throughout the 1970s and 1980s. In *Down Beat*, for example, small side-bars containing details of the instruments that star performers play began to appear in artist interviews in 1979/80; by 1982 these inserts often contained photos and took up as much as an entire half-page (in the more recent popular-music magazines such information is written directly into the interview texts themselves). During the late 1980s, *Down Beat* also added a regular column on sound equipment and new products of interest. Similarly, in July of 1985 *Keyboard* announced a 'new era' for the magazine: apparently in response to 'reader demand', it planned to expand coverage in the areas of equipment reviews and technical applications.

A characteristic common to the majority of these magazines is that they contain *only* advertising that is directly aimed at musicians; that is, one finds no ads for cigarettes, alcohol, etc. (this fact alone sets these magazines apart from large-circulation fanzines such as *Rolling Stone* or *Spin*). In 1980, *Contemporary Keyboard* magazine stated openly in an editorial that it had 'a policy of rejecting all ads that aren't music related' (Vol. 6, No. 2: 3). The same issue included, for the first time, an advertisers' index – another feature that has become characteristic of most musicians' magazines – thus assuring that the accessing of promotional information from advertisers was as easy for the readership as accessing the magazine's feature articles.[2] In later issues, as if this practice had created some special form of intimacy between advertisers, music magazines and their readers, a headline above the ad index read: 'They're in Keyboard because they care about musicians.'

A fourth element contributing to the growth in the number of musicians' magazines devoted to new technology is related to recent shifts in the electronics industry, and is as much technological as it is economic, related both to production capacity and marketing strategies. Despite the fact that most musical instruments (beginning with the hammer piano in the early nineteenth century) are today manufactured according to industrial processes, there is still a certain premium placed upon musical instruments that are handmade. Companies producing handcrafted guitars and basses (even electric ones) remain and, in the 1960s, it was common for engineers to custom-design and build mixing consoles for their own studio needs. Similarly, in the late 1960s and early 1970s, the synthesizer industry consisted of only a few small, privately owned companies; the instruments themselves bore the names of their inventors (e.g., the 'Moog' and 'Buchla' synthesizers).

But electronic instruments do not exactly lend themselves to small-scale production and, as the market expanded during the late 1970s and, more importantly, as the industry shifted to microprocessor-based technologies, a number of large Japanese corporations (such as Casio, Roland and Yamaha) began to dominate the field. The Japanese corporations (especially Casio, which gears its products more to the amateur-musician market) are closely linked to the manufacturers of integrated circuits and utilize modern production techniques (for example, Yamaha employs robotics in the manufacture of its electronic keyboards). During the early 1980s, these companies pursued an aggressive marketing strategy that sought to bring the price of digital instruments down to levels that were accessible to the average musician/consumer (see Moog, 1985: 42–4). These two elements – production capacity and marketing strategy – are clearly linked and, as Stuart Ewen (1976) has pointed out, have been an essential feature of capitalist production since the 1920s. With enhanced industrial production capacity, manufacturers increasingly need to concern themselves not only with the production of goods but, also, with the production of consumers.

It is here again that the need for musicians' magazines becomes evident, but not simply as a result of the role played, within them, by advertising. The magazines promote a whole philosophy of music-making that is based around new technology and consumption. In the past, when a musician purchased a musical instrument it was usually with the assumption that the instrument would last for years (often, musical instruments were handed down from one generation to the next); in our culture, in contrast, technology is essentially linked with notions of progress and change and, for the manufacturers of electronic musical instruments, it is important that musicians adopt these values, especially as they relate to the need for renewed consumption of goods. Such strategies have not gone unnoticed by musicians (the most prominent criticism of the new technology of the 1980s, even among its advocates, has been the excessive speed of technological change) but it is precisely in the musicians' magazines that these issues are most clearly raised and, to a certain extent, resolved.

In this sense, musicians' magazines are unique, I think (at least in relation to their speciality magazine counterparts for hi-fi enthusiasts and computer users), because the relationship between musicians and their musical instruments is such a loaded symbolic terrain: traditional values link musical instruments to romantic notions of authenticity and personal expression and, for this reason, the role of new technology in popular music has become highly contested (see Frith, 1986). Musicians' magazines play an important part in the redefinition of musical values, in renegotiating what William Leiss (1976) might call the 'material-symbolic' status of musical instruments as objects of consumption and use (see also, Jhally, 1987: 1–23).

Finally, there have been a number of factors at work within the music industry of the late 1970s and early 1980s that have had a powerful impact on the ways in which young musicians interact and pursue their career goals; these factors have, no doubt, also contributed to the increased popularity of musicians' magazines. Prior to this period, it was normal for young musicians to spend their early years learning songs from records, rehearsing with other like-minded musicians and performing in small clubs. H. Stith Bennett has described this process as three separate, though interdependent forms of interaction: a 'musician-recording interaction', a 'musician-musician interaction', and a group-audience interaction' (1980: 232).

Since the late 1970s, however, with the increased availability of inexpensive drum machines, synthesizers and sequencers, young musicians have been able to work without certain members of the band if adequate players cannot be found or, in the case of songwriters, to produce fully arranged demo tapes without the aid of outside musical collaborators. Added to this enhanced technical capability and the possibility of autonomous musical creation was the initial impact that disco music had on the availability of venues for the performance of live music in many urban centres during the late 1970s and early 1980s. (In this regard, it is interesting to note that the most significant new forms of popular music to emerge since the late 1970s have been hiphop and rap music – musical forms based around DJ/performers, phonograph turntables, studio sampling, and dance-club venues.) While the impact of this latter factor has been subject to a great deal of regional variation and seems to have changed with time (by the end of the 1980s there appears to have been a resurgence of live music venues in many centres), it is clear that the combination of these factors has placed a certain pressure on young musicians to develop their skills outside of group rehearsal and live performance contexts and to make increasing use of demo tapes in order to gain exposure to record company A & R departments. Indeed, demo production has become the preferred method of introducing new talent to record companies (bands now regularly produce demos even before they have ever played before a live audience) and greater emphasis has been placed on demos of master quality. As one A & R representative put it, the 1980s became 'the era of the competitive demo' (Kasha and Hirschhorn, 1990: 267).

The technical nature of the new instruments and recording devices ('technical' in the sense that their operation requires a form of technical knowledge that is different from traditional forms of musical knowledge and skill) has forced many musicians to rely more heavily on specialized musicians' magazines as sources of information because of the difficulty of finding local musicians with adequate knowledge of the technologies or the techniques employed in their use. Indeed, during the mid-1980s – the most intense period of technological change in recent musical instrument design – it was often necessary for even the magazine editors to seek out software developers and product specialists as authors of magazine articles on new products, as the latter were, in many cases, the only people who had adequate knowledge of all the available product features. This situation has become especially important for younger musicians, who find they can no longer rely entirely upon local networks of more experience musicians for their apprenticeship training.

In a more general sense, the music industry context has become more complex throughout the 1980s. For example, in addition to producing demo tapes, aspiring young musicians must now also confront the problems of video production. Record deals with major recording companies are increasingly made at the international level, thus rendering decisions concerning repertoire, production and management more critical and the problems of exposure more difficult. If they decide to release their own recordings, musicians must choose between a variety of competing technical formats and distribution channels. The 'how-to-make-it-in-the-music-business' type of book has long been a staple of the music publishing industry and, while such books continue to appear year after year, much of the information they contain quickly becomes outdated. The musicians' magazines have an obvious advantage in this respect in that they can provide more up-to-date information concerning such matters, and most of them devote regular features to changes within the industry, professional tips, career advice, etc. Here again, much of this information is difficult, if not impossible, for musicians to obtain at the local level from their peers.

As I have attempted to show here, a number of factors occurring simultaneously across several different industries have contributed to the recent proliferation of musicians' magazines. Nevertheless, I would argue it is becoming increasingly clear to many professional, semiprofessional and amateur musicians themselves that they now operate at increasing distances from one another and from their audiences and that they often must rely on other, more mediated forms of interaction. In this regard, musicians' magazines have come to play a role in supplying musicians with both essential information and also, perhaps, a sense of community – a community that is, however, completely integrated with their position as a market for musical instrument manufacturers.

The magazines

In turning to the magazines themselves, one is immediately struck by the sheer number and apparent diversity of these publications – by the manner in which musicians have been divided, for marketing purposes, into discreet categories of interest. The average newsstand or musical instrument shop in Montreal, for example, carries magazines devoted to keyboard players, guitarists, drummers, sound engineers and producers. In many cases, newsstands carry more than one publication in several of these catagories. For example, there are four major publications which focus primarily on synthesizer, sampler and related technology alone: two published in the United States (*Keyboard* and *Electronic Musician*), one in Britain (*Music Technology* which, until recently, also appeared in a somewhat different American edition – Canadians having the dubious honour of being able to obtain both editions) and one, a French-language publication with an English title (*Keyboards*), which is published in France.

At the 1990 summer trade show held by the National Association of Music Merchants (NAMM) in Chicago, over forty publications were on display, the majority being those devoted to specialized sectors of the musical instrument trade or consumer magazines for musicians. Given the number of periodicals in the field and their relative degree of specialization it is not surprising that their individual circulation figures are relatively small. The oldest among them, *Down Beat*, which used to think of itself as 'The Musician's Bible', has been published continuously since the era of the swing bands (since July 1934); until recently, its content has been primarily oriented towards jazz musicians and fans. In 1972, during a period when competition in the field was still relatively low, it had achieved an average circulation of over 90,000 copies per issue; in 1989, when competition was considerably stiffer and its editorial policies had changed so as to allow for coverage of a broader range of musical styles, its circulation was still only 89,000–90,000. The following list (which is by no means comprehensive) reveals the more general pattern of growth in the market during this period:

Title and date of first publication	Approx. average circulation (in NA) for the year 1989[3]
Guitar Player (1967)	132,000
Contemporary Keyboard (1975) (now *Keyboard*)	65,000
Musician (1976)	105,000
Modern Drummer (1977)	85,000
Canadian Musician (1979)	28,000
Music Technology (US edition, 1986)	50,000
Music & Sound Output (1982) (now *Stage & Studio*)	76,500
Home & Studio Recording (US ed., 1987)	50,000
Guitar, for the Practising Musician (1983)	152,500
Music, Computers & Software (1985)	56,500
Electronic Musician (1986)	77,500
Rhythm (US ed., 1988)	40,000
Modern Keyboard (1988)	65,000

In addition to these consumer magazines there are a number of periodicals directed to sound engineers and producers – such as *db*, 1967, *Recording Engineer/Producer*, 1970, *Mix*, 1977, and others – whose circulation is generally smaller than the above, ranging from approximately 20,000 to 40,000 copies. Many of these magazines belong more to the category of business publications: their circulations are mostly controlled (i.e., they are distributed, often free of charge, directly to professionals in the field) and their main revenue comes from advertising. Because they have only a limited distribution they have not been included here.

The impact of rock music on the music periodical industry (and, by extension, the musical instrument industry) is clear: the two magazines with the highest circulation are for guitarists (and there are several other guitar magazines in the field) and, ever since the introduction of synthesizers into popular music, an increase in the number of keyboard and high-technology magazines has also been evident. Still, when compared to the circulation figures of specialized hi-fi and computer magazines, which can be as high as several hundred thousand copies, the circulation of these musicians' magazines seems relatively limited. It is only when one ignores the apparent diversity (or fragmentation) of the market and looks at the field as a whole that the figures even begin to appear significant.

At the industry level, this surface diversity also serves to mask what is in actual fact a very high degree of economic concentration: many of these publications belong to 'families' of musician-oriented magazines which are published by the same interests. For example, Music Maker Publications, based in Britain, publishes both books and magazines, the latter including *Music Technology, Guitarist, Rhythm, Home & Studio Recording, Home Keyboard Review*, and *Hip-Hop Connection*. Until recently, three of these also appeared in US editions, sharing about 25 per cent of their content with their British counterparts. Similar conditions existed in the US during the 1980s with GPI Publications (publishers of *Guitar Player, Keyboard, Frets*, various books and newsletters); Mix Publications (*Mix, Electronic Musician*, and the Mix Bookshelf – a distributor of books, videos, music software and other products); and Billboard Publications (*Billboard* and, through its various divisions and subsidiaries, *Musician* magazine, books and directories).

The more successful among these enterprises became the object of takeovers by large corporate interests as the 1980s drew to a close. The GPI group was acquired by Miller Freeman Publications, a California-based company founded at the turn of the century and publisher of trade magazines for the natural-resource industries and specialized high-technology areas of the medical, computer and electronics fields. It was in turn acquired by United Newspapers, the UK media conglomerate. Mix Publications is now owned by ACT III Publishing, which also publishes magazines for the corporate-video sector and for broadcast engineers (the company itself is part of a larger media group with interests in film production, movie theatres and television broadcasting).

It is difficult to gauge the effects of industrial conglomeration of this kind in the publishing industry: while concentration of ownership has long been a concern in the area of newspaper publishing, historians of the magazine industry have generally felt that the sheer number of titles, the relative fragmentation and complexity of the market, and other factors mitigate against the possible adverse effects of conglomeration. Others, however, have observed that such forces, acting in the area of special-interest magazines in one particular field, may result in a reduction in the number of available titles (see Taft, 1982: 287) and something of this kind may be beginning to take place in the field of musicians' magazines. Faced with stiff competition from its rivals in the US (and a general downturn in the synthesizer market as the 1990s got under way) Music Maker Publications has been forced to allow its US edition of *Music Technology* to suspend independent operations and to be absorbed by its more successful US publication, *Home & Studio Recording*. Later, in the fall of 1990, Music Maker entered into an agreement in which Miller Freeman would take over the publication of *Rhythm* (US) while continuing to share some of its editorial content with the UK edition.

The level of concentration within this specialized area of publishing may also affect relations between the publishers and the industry they serve, as well as having an impact on the general character of the magazines themselves. For example, in Canada, where the market is very small and already dominated by foreign publications, there are relatively few Canadian periodicals serving the popular music industry. As already mentioned above, the Toronto-based Norris Publications publishes both *Canadian Musician* (a magazine which attempts to cross over the boundary between a magazine aimed mainly at musicians and one aimed at a more general readership interested in Canadian music) and *Canadian Music Trade* (a business magazine distributed primarily to musical instrument retailers). Norris also planned to launch a new magazine for sound engineers in the fall of 1990 called *Professional Sound*. Perhaps even more significant than simple ownership is the fact that all three magazines share the same editorial and production staff. Norris also has interests in book publishing (music books and an industry directory) and artist management. In the Canadian situation, then, Norris Publications and its affiliates have become a singular, multifunction management, promotion and information vehicle linking several sectors within the industry – from instruments manufacturers and distributors to retailers, artists and consumers.

In contrast, most of the magazines published outside Canada have separate editorial boards and fewer direct links with the instrument or music industries. Nevertheless, a large number of editors and contributors from the magazines have, on occasion or in regular featured articles, appeared in the pages of their so-called 'sister' publications or in magazines by different (i.e., competing) publishers. Several current editors and other writers have also contributed to (or, in some cases, worked for) manufacturer-sponsored publications or user-group newsletters, written technical manuals or served as consultants for instrument manufacturers, or developed sound programs for new electronic musical instruments. One prominent writer claimed that he could never be accused of conflict of interest because he had worked, at one time or another, for just about everyone in the business; this, apparently, was a guarantee that he was not beholden to anyone.

The net result of such economic and intellectual concentration is a certain homogeneity in general style, outlook, and approach between the various publications. This approach was neatly summed up in the editorial page of the recent inaugural issue of *Bass Player* magazine:

> Our goal is simple: to provide electronic and acoustic bassists with the information they need to become better players, more successful musicians, and more savvy consumers of equipment (Spring, 1990: 4).

Canadian Musician (perhaps because of its crossover orientation) put it somewhat differently: 'We cover the People ... the Business ... the Products' (Promotional brochure, 1990). The elements are the same: star performers and musicianship, business and careers, and, above all, products. Indeed, the two former elements are ultimately collapsed into the latter:

> In today's business, the musician's tools – from instruments to recording technology – can make or break a song. *Canadian Musician*'s regular product reports give detailed analysis of some of the latest technology – once again, by people using it on current projects (Promotional brochure, 1990).

It should perhaps be noted here, if only in passing, that this emphasis on new musical products has not been limited to the pop/rock sectors of the musical world alone. Rather, it appears to have been a widespread side-effect of the increased speed of technological innovation and high-intensity marketing strategies in the musical instrument industry of the 1980s. The *Computer Music Journal*, published by MIT Press, is one of the most prestigious forums of avant-garde electronic music; it publishes only the most specialized, learned articles on the mathematics, theories, techniques and aesthetics of digital sound production. Because of the technical nature of the field the journal has, since its inception in 1977, always included a short 'Products of Interest' column and, from about 1979 onwards, began to accept a limited number of advertisements from selected manufacturers; during the early years, the column and the ads together seldom contributed more than a couple of pages to the length of the journal.

Both sections expanded considerably during the 1980s, however. In 1985, Yamaha took out a two-page display ad at the back of the journal, and, by 1988, the ads and product reviews often exceeded thirty pages in length, constituting over one-third of the total content of the journal. These trends parallel, quite closely, similar developments in the popular-musicians' magazines, despite the fact that advertising content tends, on average, to be higher in the latter, amounting, on average, to 50 per cent of the total magazine pages. Even the tone of the reviews in the *Computer Music Journal* sometimes approached that of the popular magazines, as in references to how much 'bang for the buck' a particular product offered. In this regard, there would seem to be little difference between the avant-garde's fascination with technology and that of the pop musician.

What still separates the academic computer-music journal from the pop magazines, however, is the degree to which content can be separated from advertising messages. The articles and interviews found in most popular-musicians' magazines place a heavy emphasis on the equipment musicians use and, as in those ads that use star endorsements, an almost elementary process of transferal takes place whereby the attitudes and values attributed to the artist are transferred to the objects of consumption. (In this regard, musicians are not different from any other fan; they are just as susceptible to the blandishments of the star system as anyone else.) Again, whatever claims to integrity the avant-garde might have does not make them immune to this process; in an interview with Laurie Anderson, a photo caption reads: 'Armed with a Roland D-50 and a challenging view of society, Anderson wails at the Brooklyn Academy of Music in 1988' (*Keyboard*, December 1989: 75). In this sense, contemporary musicians' magazines offer prime examples confirming Andrew Wernick's description of the media in a 'promotional culture': 'thematically, ideologically and stylistically, the non-advertising content comes to be angled and coded in terms of the same economically functional categories as those which substructure the ads themselves' (1985: 14). Conversely, ads sometimes disguise themselves as interviews and product reviews and must be labelled, in small print, as advertisements by the magazine editors.

These observations suggest that any discursive analysis of musicians' magazines would have to avoid any strict, conventional categorizations or discursive typologies in favour of an analysis that seeks common procedures that cut across all boundaries and types (see Finlay-Pelinsky, 1983). In the hi-tech magazines, both the advertisements and the feature articles emphasize various technical discourses, especially those concerned with power and control. But what is perhaps most interesting for my argument here is the manner in which the discursive practices of 'futurology' (Finlay-Pelinsky, 1983: 18–22) come to serve these magazines in their attempts to stimulate the consumption of new technology. This was especially prominent during the latter part of 1989 and the beginning of 1990, when many of the magazines attempted to sum up the technical achievements of the 1980s and to assess the possibilities for the 1990s. All seemed to agree that the pace of technical innovation had been too rapid during the 1980s, that a slow-down was welcome and that musicians needed time to learn to use the instruments that they already had. But then, as they turned to the 1990s, all the ills of the past decade appeared to be magically resolved by the promise of the new technologies of the future. It is this constant forward looking – this deferral of pleasure and satisfaction into the future – that contributes to the sense of desire and need that is necessary if the pace of technical innovation (and profits) is to be kept at a maximum.

As discussed earlier, however, the area of musical instruments is a highly contested territory and not all musicians are readily inclined to rally behind the futurist call for newer, ever more powerful technologies. Not unlike the world of classical music, where the fetish for old instruments places an excessive monetary and symbolic value on Stradivarius violins and the like, many pop musicians have a special reverence for guitars and amplifiers of a certain make, model and year – for a particular Stratocaster or Les Paul guitar, for example, or for old tube amplifiers of the 1960s. In the world of hi-tech, digital musical instruments, something similar exists in the romance with 'warm' analog synthesizer sounds of the 1970s. Andrew Goodwin has argued that to play an analog synth 'is now a mark of authenticity, where it was once a sign of alienation' (1988: 45). *Keyboard* magazine has even introduced a regular addition to its instructional columns entitled 'Vintage Synths'.

There is, nevertheless, something strange about this sudden historical interest on the part of magazines that regularly publish buyer's guides with feature-by-feature comparisons of the latest and the 'hottest' gear on the market. It seems to me that this interest in bestowing 'vintage' status upon technically (if not musically) obsolete instruments of the past functions somewhat differently in this context than it does in the case of other musical instruments. In effect, the magazines are saying to consumers, 'Yes, you *can* buy that new synthesizer, sampler or drum machine because it *will* still be worth something several years from now.' And at least one reviewer has expressed exactly those sentiments:

> I firmly believe this will be among the last generation of drum machines ... Certainly, I can see it being the kind of machine people will be desperate to get their hands on in 1995, or whenever nostalgia for good old 1989 becomes fashionable. We're talking investment opportunities here. (Nigel Lord, in *Rhythm*, November 1989: 55)

In this way, the discourse of 'vintage' instruments is a strategic one: it helps to counteract the fear among many consumers of new technology that their purchases will become obsolescent and worthless.

Furthermore, as is made clear in the reviewer's comments, the fetish of older musical instruments is essentially a nostalgic one: 'vintage' instruments are understood to give the player a form of direct sonic (and sometimes iconic) access to the past and, thereby, an almost magical ability to evoke the power of some past music. And, in this sense, there is a curious kind of 'fit' between technological 'progress' in musical instruments and recording equipment in the post-war period and the dominant modes in which popular music is produced, distributed and consumed. Nostalgia is coded into the lyrics of many pop songs – 'Remember when ...', 'She's gone', etc. – and into their structure (in devices such as the fade-out). DJ patter and mainstream radio formats frame popular music in terms of the passage of time – 'Contemporary Hits', 'Golden Oldies', 'Classic Rock'. And, among the various ways in which popular music functions for the listener is the manner in which it helps to organize our sense of the present and the past, our notions of youth and adolescence. In the age of electronic reproduction, sounds themselves have become an increasingly important part of the way in which musical genres and the passage of time are coded. Musicians' magazines play a critical role in this process by helping musicians to define the various relationships between sounds, musical styles and the passage of time – they help to define those sounds which are truly 'new', those which, through over-use, have become merely stale, and those which have become the signs of a nostalgic past.[4]

Another issue raised briefly earlier in this essay concerned the context in which some musicians may have come to rely on magazines as a particular form of mediated interaction. In this regard, it is interesting to explore the manner in which the musicians' magazines themselves work to simultaneously construct their readers as both a kind of musical 'community' and a market. They do this in a number of ways. Firstly, many of the magazines hold yearly readers' polls, typically in a 'vox-pop' style (i.e., readers are asked to choose, from among a select group of star performers, who they think is the best jazz or new-age synthesist, rock guitarist, classical pianist, etc.). Such events offer the readers a chance to 'vote', and to thereby gain a sense of authority and competence from their ability to choose (in part, because it is a process in which they reaffirm the choices they have already made when purchasing recordings). At the same time, these polls both offer the magazine a chance to address the readers as a kind of pseudo 'public' and allow them to obtain information that can be useful in planning future interviews and articles. *Keyboard* magazine (then known as *Contemporary Keyboard*) made use of this type of polling during the mid-1970s, shortly after it began publication. By the early 1980s, however, *Keyboard* was engaged in a different kind of polling, one more focused on probing into the personal habits of this 'body politic'. Since that time, readers have been regularly asked to respond to questions concerning their age, sex, income, interest in the magazine, the kind of instruments they owned and, more importantly, how much money they were likely to spend on their *next* purchase and the kind of instrument it was likely to be.

The shift to this type of information-gathering is as significant for what it says about the changing function of the magazines themselves as it is for what it reveals about their readership. These surveys would seem to indicate a shift away from an ideology involving the representation of a readership, a 'public', towards one more clearly based on supplying marketing information to advertisers. The stated aim of the surveys is to 'monitor current consumer trends, and to anticipate their future needs and buying habits', 'to gather valid data on the technology-based music instrument market', and to provide advertisers with 'unique insights' that will allow them 'to better position their products and services in the mind of the consumer' (advertisers' report, *Trends in Technology II*, 1990: 3).

In an as-yet incomplete series of interviews that I have been conducting with individuals associated with instrument manufacturing and musicians' magazines, one publisher responded with the following remarks when asked whether his magazine was 'advertiser-led':

> We write for the readers, not for the industry . . . we're not advertiser led, nor product led. We are selling a readership to advertisers so our main aim is to develop and maintain a readership. (Publisher, personal interview)

For him, there appeared to be no conflict whatsoever between the requirements of writing *for* a readership and simultaneously selling it to advertisers. Others have told me that conflicts often arise when manufacturers attempt to have the amount of editorial content devoted to their products tied to the amount of advertising dollars spent in the magazine; all deny that their own magazines bow to such pressure but suggest that other, less scrupulous editors do.

For their part, some of the manufacturers seem to feel that the magazines do not co-operate enough with them in their marketing efforts. At the trade shows – those semi-annual rituals where the industry meets face to face – there have been incidents where manufacturers berated magazine editors for adopting a flippant or arrogant attitude towards reviewing their products. Ultimately, however, the industry knows it must accept bad reviews along with good ones, for, as Chapple and Garofalo have noted in their discussion of the record industry and the music press, what really matters is the implicit promise that the products will indeed be covered (1977: 165–6). At the same time, whatever credibility with their readership magazines may gain through their apparent honesty is then used by the manufacturers when they reproduce (with the permission of the magazines) the reviews of their products for distribution in musical instrument shops. The more 'objective' the review, the more effective the promotional tool.

As for the community of readers themselves, the surveys reveal that they are largely young and almost exclusively male (as high as 98 per cent of those responding to readership surveys for magazines devoted to new technologies), the latter fact reflecting the more general male domination of production in popular music and, more specifically, the male orientation of technical culture. In editorials, the magazines all appear to be critical of this state of affairs and thereby attempt to absolve themselves of any responsibility in the matter, but even a cursory look at the division of labour within the magazines, their editorial and advertising content, or the discourses and modes of address used in the construction and sharing of technical knowledge reveal a definition of technology and musicianship which is highly gendered.

While it is beyond the scope of this paper to pursue these questions in detail, it seems worth mentioning that the overriding feature of female involvement in the world of musicians' magazines is their near-total absence. Within the division of labour in the magazines themselves, the vast majority of the senior editors and the regular contributors are male, with women most often occupying positions as editorial assistants, designers on the production staff, or as marketing and sales reps, etc. – positions of low visibility (to the readership) which allow those who occupy them little opportunity to speak for themselves or for their magazines. In this respect, popular musicians' magazines constitute an area wherein males retain a monopoly on speech.

An absence of female performers is also evident in magazine content: by the end of 1989, after fifteen years of publishing (a total of over 160 issues), *Keyboard* had devoted its cover story to only a handful of select, female artists: among them, Wendy Carlos (a transsexual, born Walter), Kate Bush and Laurie Anderson. The track record for the other magazines is generally no better but the magazines with the highest commitment to new technology, such as *Electronic Musician* or *Home & Studio Recording*, tend to avoid the issue entirely by not putting people on their covers at all. By displacing people with technology, all social ills seem to disappear into the glossy surface of the technical objects themselves. (The magazine editors and marketing representatives generally feel that photographs emphasizing 'hardware' and copy dealing with technical specifications are gender-neutral).

Even more intriguing, perhaps, is the manner in which new technology and technical production activity is portrayed with respect to its colonization of the private sphere. The home has been the traditional site of female music-making, but, as the magazines have turned their attention to developing the notion of the 'home studio', there has been a noticeable lack of female (or family) participation in this project. The so-called 'electronic cottage' has been located, or so it would seem, in a remarkably deserted terrain.

On those rare occasions when the magazines have attempted to tackle the question of gender in the musicians' community, however, it is again interesting to see the manner in which such questions are immediately linked to issues of marketing. A guest editorial written by Marsha Vdovin (marketing director for a software company) and published in *Electronic Musician* (November 1989: 130) raised the problem of how women have been 'discouraged from technological paths'. Typically, however, the most convincing argument that she could muster as to why women should be welcomed into the technological community was not that they stood to benefit individually or as a group from such a development, but that 'they represent a market of amazing potential' and that marketing people should use tools such as advertising to 'both *create* and tap into' this market (Vdovin's emphasis). This fusion of arguments concerning technology, economy and social equity is not unique to questions of gender; rather, it has long been associated with discourses that centre around notions of 'democratization' and technology.

Musicians' magazines also attempt to create a sense of community by adopting terms and strategies that are characteristic of more traditional rituals of musician interaction: for example, regular articles dealing with musical technique in magazines such as *Keyboard* are titled 'Private Lessons', thus invoking a traditional sense of musician apprenticeship. *Keyboard* also makes extensive use of musical notation in many of its articles and regularly carries transcriptions of popular songs; in this way, the editors make certain assumptions about the musical training of their readers and place the magazine firmly within the range of activities – Bennett's 'musician-recording' and 'musician-musician' interactions – described earlier as typical among popular musicians. *Electronic Musician*, on the other hand, seldom makes use of traditional notation and, instead of transcriptions and lessons in musical technique, instructs its readers in how to build electronic devices and how to write computer software (thus reflecting its roots in the tradition of hobbyist magazines such as *Popular Electronics*). Such divergences in approach are not only significant in terms of the readership they attract but, more importantly, in the way in which they define two very different kinds of activity as meaningful forms of musical behaviour.

Divergences of this kind are also evident in the editorial attitude taken towards the relationship between conventional musical skills and new technology. In response to recent reports concerning the spread of lip-syncing in live performance contexts, one magazine editor espoused the virtues of live performance and 'the level of human interaction that only real-time singing and playing can provide'. Continuing, he pleaded with his readers that they not get 'lost in the search for perfection... Reach for your potential as a performer and do the best you can with the gear you've got' (Scott Wilkinson in *Home & Studio Recording*, July 1990: 76). A few months later, taking an opposing stance, *Electronic Musician* published a guest editorial that referred to performing musicians as mere 'technicians' and decried the necessity of 'spending several years learning (and maintaining) the specialized skills required to play a musical instrument'. The solution to this dilemma was to be found in the search for new technology:

> Manufacturers should make an effort to appeal to the composer in us all ... there are those of us who are more interested in and able to work with the overall shape and feel of a composition than the details that comprise it ...... Let's envision instruments and software aimed at the composer instead of the technician. (Chris Meyer in *Electronic Musician*, September 1990: 114)

Interestingly, the more moderate, integrationist argument is offered as the personal opinion of the editor and makes its appeal to the reader on the basis of traditional notions of musical skill. The radical, techno-utopian vision, on the other hand, adopts a mode of address that makes constant use of the third-person pronouns 'we' and 'us' and contains an explicit call for the increased production and consumption of goods. In this way, the author invites his readers to join in this call for the development of new, innovative technologies, thereby contributing to both the formation of a market and the creation of a sense of communal ideals.

The sharing of knowledge in less formalized settings than that of the private lesson is also typical of local communities of musicians. In this regard, the conventional ritual wherein pop musicians share new 'licks' they have learned is reflected in the technical magazines' regular columns devoted to synthesizer sound 'patches' submitted by readers. The prerequisite for participation in these mediated rituals is, of course, that one owns one of the synthesizers in question. Technology becomes, in this sense, the communal bond itself.

This idea – that technology has become the bond that ties – is the implicit, guiding assumption that pervades much of the content of the new musicians' magazines. In the same way that musicians have always identified themselves in terms of the instruments they play, the magazines now refer to this new community of musicians as 'electronic musicians' or 'recording musicians'. But whereas subtle differences of class, taste, and musical style are still conveyed by the appellation 'violinist' as opposed to 'fiddler', these new terms appeal to a kind of universality – they make no claim to any stylistic or regional difference. This general attitude is perhaps most explicitly demonstrated in an advertisement that appeared last year celebrating the success of the Korg M1 synthesizer:

> In less than a year, the M1 has become more than the world's best-selling keyboard. It has become a form of communication. A universal tool allowing everyone in the creative process of music to exchange new sounds. Develop ideas. And collaborate on projects ... [the M1 is] creating a worldwide network of professionals who are bringing about changes in music faster than ever before.... And with the number of M1 products – and users – growing every day, you can imagine the potential of such a universal language. Just think, then, how great your potential will be once you begin to speak it. (Korg product ad, in *Electronic Musician*, Vol. 5, No. 5, 1989: 3)

Thus, technology has replaced music in the old bourgeois myth of the 'universal language' – indeed, technology has become transparent, 'a form of communication', 'language' itself. If one learns to 'speak' technology (that is, if one becomes a consumer of technological products – a 'user', one is immediately admitted, or so it would seem, into that international fraternity of musicians, the 'worldwide network of professionals'. In a musical world where it has become difficult for the aspiring young musician to have meaningful interactions with other musicians and with audiences, where it has become difficult to even secure a gig at a local club, the myth of technology is, no doubt, a powerful force with which to contend.

Conclusion

The 1980s witnessed an enormous growth in the innovation, diffusion and use of digital musical instruments in the production of popular music. This phenomenon was supported by the rise of various user groups, information networks and, especially, commercial magazines devoted to musicians and technicians; indeed, without the simultaneous growth of the musicians' magazine industry, it is unlikely that this phenomenon would have achieved anywhere near the magnitude that it has today. (By the late 1980s, the production of digital musical instruments had become a multibillion dollar industry.)

In several of my discussions with the publishers and editors of these magazines I have found that they recognize the role they have played: they feel that they have not only reflected the musical and technical trends manifest during this period but, as well, that they have helped to establish those trends in the first place. Indeed, when, in July 1988, *Electronic Musician* published a special issue on the previous twenty years of achievements in musical electronics, one of those 'achievements' included the launching of a newsletter called *Electronotes* – a publication which, according to *Electronic Musician*, played a critical role in the development of electronic musical instruments during the 1970s. But it is the combined influence of these two publications that is perhaps most significant. Their influence is not unlike that of the early photography magazines described by Howard Becker (1982: 314–17): *Electronotes* belongs to that category of publications that grow out of the need for experimenters to communicate with one another in order to define the nature of new technical possibilities. Magazines such as *Electronic Musician*, on the other hand, appear at a later stage and are more geared towards promotion and consumption, their main purpose being to help users to *learn* the specific pleasures offered by the new technical medium. In this regard, the publishers and editors also realize the power that they wield within the musical instrument industry. As one publisher put it, 'the industry recognizes that we are the link between them and the market' (personal interview).

Nevertheless, as I have attempted to argue here, this phenomenon has taken place both within a high-intensity market context and in a context in which musicians have been compelled, for a variety of reasons, to operate at increasing distances from one another and from their audiences. In this sense, musicians' magazines have perhaps become, not only a link between the musicians and the industry, but, as well, an essential mediating factor in 'musician-musician interactions'. This double mediation contributes to their simultaneous construction as both a community and a market.

Peterson has stated that the creation of a 'cultural bond' and a sense of 'national community' has been an important characteristic of magazine publishing in the United States throughout the twentieth century (1964: 449). The development of national magazine publishing itself complemented an expansion in the manufacturing and distribution of consumer goods that took place at the turn of the century. But in the context of an increasing internationalization of commodity production, the logic of the 'cultural bond' has perhaps changed: the formation of a sense of community takes place within specialized consumer groups whose frame of reference is less national than international, less bound to a sense of shared 'perspective' than to a bond with commodities themselves.

Thus, musicians' magazines today play a critical role in the mediation of human needs through objects. New musical technology has been reified as the tie that binds a community of musicians together while, at the same time, it is the object of consumption whose success in the market-place is essential to the survival of the electronic instrument industry. In the final analysis there is a double production going on: one industry produces technology, the other produces consumers.

Notes

1 *Rolling Stone* has been published continuously since 1967 and, during the past decade, has regularly achieved circulation figures of over one million copies.
2 Interestingly enough, the pop/rock magazines were not the first in the area of music periodical publishing to include advertiser indexes; in the educational field – the primary market for band instrument manufacturers – publications such as

the *Music Educator's Journal* have contained similar indexes since at least the mid-1960s.

3 Circulation figures are rounded to the nearest 500; they are taken, for the most part, from *The Standard Periodical Directory* and *Ulrich's International Periodicals Directory*. In some cases, figures were obtained from the magazine publishers themselves or from audited statements (ABC or BPA) when these were made available to me. Although figures in the two main directories are supposed to be from audited sources, there seems to be considerable variation between them for individual titles: for example, *Electronic Musician* is listed in *Standard* with a circulation of 77,500 but in *Ulrich's* the figure is only 65,000. There may be a number of reasons for these discrepancies but the figures quoted here are, to my knowledge, reasonably accurate.

4 I would like to thank Ottawa guitarist, Don Wallace, for prompting me to consider some of the possible implications of the 'vintage' instrument phenomenon in popular music.

References

Anonymous (1980) *Canadian Advertising Rates & Data*, 63 (10), October.
Anonymous (1990) *CARD Publication Profiles '91*, (10), September.
Anonymous (1990) *Standard Periodical Directory* (For US and Canada). New York: Oxbridge.
Anonymous (1990–1) *Ulrich's International Periodicals Directory* (29th edition). New York: Reed Publishing.
Becker, Howard S. (1982) *Art Worlds*. Berkeley: University of California Press.
Bennett, H. Stith (1980) 'The realities of practice', in Frith and Goodwin (1990): 221–37.
—— (1983) 'Notation and identity in contemporary popular music', *Popular Music* 3: 215–34.
Chambers, Iain (1985) *Urban Rhythms*. London: Macmillan.
Chapple, Steve and Garofalo, Reebee (1977) *Rock 'n' Roll is Here to Pay*. Chicago: Nelson-Hall.
Dougherty, Philip H. (1986) 'Trade ads aid sales study says', *New York Times*, 16 October 1986: D22.
Draper, Robert (1990) *Rolling Stone Magazine: The Uncensored History*. New York: Doubleday.
Ewen, Stuart (1976) *Captains of Consciousness: Advertising and the Social Roots of the Consumer Culture*. New York: McGraw-Hill.
Feld, Steven (1984) 'Communication, music, and speech about music', *Yearbook for Traditional Music*, 16: 1–18.
Finlay-Pelinsky, Marike (1983) 'Technologies of technology: a critique of procedures of power and social control in discourses on new communications technology', in *Working Papers in Communications*. Montreal: McGill University.
Flippo, Chet (1974) 'The history of Rolling Stone', *Popular Music and Society* 3: 159–88, 258–80, 281–98.
Ford, James L. C. (1969) *Magazines for Millions: The Story of Specialized Publications*. Carbondale: Southern Illinois University Press.
Frith, Simon (1981) *Sound Effects*. New York: Pantheon.
—— (1986) 'Art versus technology: the strange case of popular music', *Media, Culture and Society* 8 (3) 263–79.

Frith, Simon and Goodwin, Andrew (1990) editors, *On Record: Rock, Pop and the Written Word*. New York: Pantheon.

Goodwin, Andrew (1988) 'Sample and hold: pop music in the digital age of reproduction', *Critical Quarterly* 30 (3): 34–49.

Ifedi, Fidelis (1990) 'Periodicals published in Canada', *Focus on Culture* 2 (1): 1–3. Ottawa: Statistics Canada, 87–104.

Jhally, Sut (1987) *The Codes of Advertising: Fetishism and the Political Economy of Meaning in the Consumer Society*. London: Frances Pinter.

Kasha, Al and Hirschhorn, Joel (1990) *If They Ask You, You Can Write a Song* (Updated ed.). New York: Fireside/Simon & Schuster.

Laing, Dave (1985) *One Chord Wonders*. Milton Keynes: Open University.

Leiss, William (1976) 'Commodities', in Leiss, *The Limits to Satisfaction: An essay on the problem of needs and commodities*. Toronto: University of Toronto Press: 71–92.

Moog, Bob (1985) 'The keyboard explosion: ten amazing years of music technology', *Keyboard* 11 (10): 36–48.

Peterson, Theodore (1964) *Magazines in the Twentieth Century*. Urbana: University of Illinois Press.

Taft, William H. (1982) *American Magazines for the 1980s*. New York: Hastings House.

Thornton, Sarah (1990) 'Strategies for reconstructing the popular past', *Popular Music* 9 (1): 87–95.

Vdovin, Marsha (1989) 'How to double the size of the music business', *Electronic Musician* 5 (11): 130.

Wernick, Andrew (1985) 'Promotional culture', paper given at a joint conference session of the Canadian Communication Association and the *Canadian Journal of Political & Social Theory*, Montreal, June 2.

MAIN PERIODICALS CONSULTED (ACCESS TO ALL OR MOST BACK ISSUES)

Canadian Musician
Canadian Music Trades
Computer Music Journal
Down Beat
Electronic Musician
Keyboard (formally *Contemporary Keyboard*)

SECONDARY PERIODICALS CONSULTED (INCOMPLETE HOLDINGS)

db, The Sound Engineering Magazine; *Recording Engineer/Producer*; *Home & Studio Recording* (US & UK editions); *Music Technology* (US & UK editions).

OTHER MUSICIAN-ORIENTED AND MUSIC INDUSTRY PERIODICALS SURVEYED

Bam, LA's Music Magazine; *Bass Player*; *Billboard*; *Clavier*; *DJ Times*; *Electronic Music Educator*; *EQ*; *Guitar Player*; *Hip-Hop Connection*; *Home Keyboard Review*; *Key Issues* (Peavey Electronics Corp.); *The IMA Bulletin*; *Instrumentalist*; *International Musician and Recording World*; *MIDI Magazine* (Atari Corp.);

Mix; *Mix Mag*; *Modern Drummer*; *Modern Keyboard*; *The Music & Computer Educator*; *Music & Sound Retailer*; *Music, Computers & Software*; *Music Educator's Journal*; *Music Inc.*; *Music Market Canada*; *The Music Paper*; *The Music Trades*; *Musical Merchandise Review*; *Musician*; *New Musical Express*; *Roland News Link* and *Roland Users Group* (Roland Corp.); *Rhythm*; *Rolling Stone*; *Spin*; *Stage & Studio*; *Street Sound*; *Transoniq Hacker*; *Up Beat Daily*.

PERSONAL INTERVIEWS (1989–90)

Frank Alkyer, Editorial Director, *Down Beat, Music Inc., Up Beat Daily*.
Craig Anderton, Founding Editor, *Electronic Musician*.
Charles C. Baake, Senior Vice-President, Miller Freeman Publications; Group Publisher, The GPI Group (*Guitar Player*, *Keyboard*, and others).
Terry Day, President, Music Maker Publications (*Music Technology, Home & Studio Recording, Rhythm*, and others).
Vanessa Else, former Senior Editor, *Electronic Musician*.
David Henman, Editor, *Canadian Music Trades, Canadian Musician*.
Jerry Kovarsky, Director of Marketing, Ensoniq Corporation.
John Maher, Publisher, *Down Beat*.
Thomas A. Sheehan, General Manager, Yamaha Communication Center.
Bob O'Donnell, Editor, *Electronic Musician* (former Editor, *Music Technology*, US edition).
Steve Oppenheimer, Associate Editor, *Electronic Musician*.
Steve Wigginton, Director of Circulation, ACT III Publishing (*Electronic Musician, Mix*, and others)
Scott Wilkinson, Editor-in-Chief, *Home & Studio Recording* (former Editor *Music Technology*).

Paul Théberge teaches in the Department of Communications Studies at Concordia University, Montreal

PAUL RUTTEN

LOCAL POPULAR MUSIC ON THE NATIONAL AND INTERNATIONAL MARKETS

One of the most notable developments in the world's popular music in the post-war era has been the growing internationalization of its sound. Those musical genres which, indisputably, have left the strongest mark on popular music in the world have originated in the United States of America and, to a lesser extent, the United Kingdom. The first of these was mainstream American jazz, which became popular in Western European countries in the 1930s and 1940s, was picked up by local musicians and then had a significant influence on local popular music scenes. Subsequent developments, like the advent of rock 'n' roll, rock, soul, funk, disco, rap, hiphop and house in the United States and 'beat' and punk musics in the United Kingdom have had a substantial impact on the continental Western European music scene.

The prominent position of the United States as a global cultural trendsetter can be traced back to changes in power relationships during and after World War II, changes which produced a situation in which 'Americana' became the model for the Western world in general. The United States embodied, for most Western European countries, a young, modern, free and industrializing country, one which provided the perfect developmental model for Continental countries then in chaos. Moreover, American culture turned out to be an attractive alternative to those things the 'old' European culture had to offer, especially to European youth. Older, European structures for the 'production of culture', consisting primarily of organizations established along ideological and mainly religious lines, were not capable of meeting the 'demands' of people living in a modern industrialized society in which the electronic mass media had become the main providers of everyday culture. American entertainment products conquered the European continent as an integral part of the American lifestyle, marketed by a cultural industry whose products, most notably movies and popular, recorded music, were new and American.

For the most part, European cultural industries have been organized along the lines of the American model. In the music, movie and print industries, the market became the dominant factor shaping production and distribution. However, the organization of broadcasting in Western European countries represented a compromise of sorts between the old and new forces within specific national contexts. In almost every European country, the state played an active role in the organization of the radio and television landscape by establishing some sort of public broadcasting, which, in many cases, was the only form of broadcasting available. In recent years, European broadcasting systems have come under pressure from corporate capital seeking to introduce commercial broadcasting into Europe. Developments over the last few years indicate that this pressure has been successful: commercial broadcasting is gaining ground in many European countries.

As far as the music industry is concerned, the market has been the dominant factor in production and distribution from the very beginning, in Europe as well as in the United States. Moreover, the scope of activities of the music industry has always been very international. For the Dutch music industry, for instance, the recording and marketing of local artists has, throughout that industry's development, been only one of its activities. At present, the principal activity of Dutch recording firms – both majors and independents – is that of distributing and marketing foreign, mainly American product.

This article is mainly concerned with discussing the position of local popular music within national and international markets, taking the Dutch situation as a starting point. 'Position' refers here to the economic viability of local music in the context of structures for the production and distribution of music operating on the national and international levels. The use of the concept 'local popular music' presupposes a specific relationship between a certain spatial context described as local and a certain kind of popular music. The relationship between the local and the music is very often conceived of in terms of notions of the indigenous, such that local music is seen as a static cultural-musical form said to be historically rooted in a specific local context. This prescriptive definition robs popular music of two of its main characteristics: its dynamism and its intertextuality. The concept of a local, popular music used here refers to a dynamic cultural practice through which people living in a specific spatial context engage in the production and reproduction of popular music. This cultural practice encompasses musical composition, the playing of music and its live performance on stage, and getting music recorded on phonograms, played over the radio, and, finally, into shops. Conceiving of the politics of local, popular music in this way links it to issues having to do with mass communication, culture and democracy, and away from the politics of a narrow-minded cultural nationalism.

The position of local music defined in these terms refers, then, to the viability of specific cultural practices within the context of a modern industrialized society where the market is the principal force shaping production and distribution. In this respect, the 'viability' of a musical practice refers to its commercial value. This value depends on the extent to which the music industries can expect to recoup their investments in musical product and eventually generate profits from selling it on the national and international market. Irrespective of the specific qualities of each individual musical piece, the commercial value of local music is largely determined by the structure of the national and international music market. Relevant factors in this context include the size of the home market, the share occupied by local music within the home market relative to that of music from abroad, and the importance of this local music on the international scene.

International market developments

Before turning to a comparative analysis of the situation of several national markets, some observations should be made concerning the changing situation within the international market. One current development with potential long-term implications is a decline in the relative importance of the American phonogram market on the one hand, and a growth in the importance of the Western European and Japanese markets on the other. The principal causes for this shift are a decline in the value of the American dollar, as well as the relatively higher growth-rates of the phonogram markets in Western European and Japan compared to that within the United States. Given the recent economic opening of Eastern Europe to the music industry, the importance of the whole of Europe as a market for the music industry will likely increase even more in the future. This development may possibly lead to a thorough reordering of the structure of the international music market, and, as a result, to significant changes in the policies of the international music industry, with as-yet uncertain consequences for the international popular soundscape.

Table 1 compares the share of the US, Western European and Japanese markets in 1984 and 1989 relative to the total world market.[1]

Table 1. Share of the turnover on the world phonogram market for different regions in 1984 and 1989

	1984 %	1989 %
Western Europe	31	41
United States	45	34
Japan	13	16
Rest of the world	11	9
Total	100	100

Data for Table 1 taken from Hung and Morencos (1990).

There are essentially two possible reactions by the music industry to the developments just described. The first is the investment of more money in domestic European and Japanese artists so as to generate profits within their domestic markets. This option was recently put forward by the president of MCA Music, Al Teller:

> For all the obvious reasons, ultimately MCA will have to participate in domestic repertoire throughout the world. . . . Right now, fundamentally we are dependent on the English language for our product. We don't enjoy the benefits of local artists selling enormous quantities of records in their territories. To be competitive with the other worldwide majors at some point we have to tap into local repertoire. That is certainly an important item on our agenda as we look out into the future internationally. . . . It is just human nature at work here. You know people love their hometown heroes. The industry could not possibly be as healthy if all the big sales came from artists who came from distant shores. In America people love it when an artist from their local city makes good. Why shouldn't the same thing be true here? I think it is important that German artists should be able to sell enormous quantities in Germany, and the same thing for French artists in France. You'll never get a healthy industry without that.[2]

The second option is to go for expanded sales of internationally-established – mainly English and American – artists. This option has been the strategy of Warner Music in the Netherlands for some years now. Warner decided to end investment in Dutch domestic artists some time ago, and to concentrate on the distribution and marketing of foreign, mainly Anglo-American repertoire within the Dutch market.

The present crisis within the American economy has made the American music industry vulnerable. This has resulted in a series of takeovers of American music companies, by Japanese and, to a lesser extent, European companies. Recent examples include the takeover of the music division of CBS by Sony. After MCA took over Geffen, it was itself acquired by another Japanese electronics company, Mitsushita. One of the bigger American independent companies, A&M Records, was bought by Dutch Polygram, which also bought the English independent Island. Industry rumours suggest that Japanese hardware companies, such as Pioneer and Toshiba, are eager to acquire or purchase a substantial stake in Warner Music. This development will, ultimately, lead to a situation in which Anglo-American music is distributed and sold all over the world by companies which were formerly American and are now Japanese. The one billion dollar deal by Sony Music (formerly CBS) with Michael Jackson is another sign of the willingness of Japanese capital to invest heavily in American popular culture.

Local music and national markets: four sorts of relationship

Three structural parameters largely determine the position of a specific local music:

1. The size of the local music market.
2. The share of local music within the overall turnover of the local music market.

3 The importance of local music within the international music market, expressed as the share of local musics within the turnover of music on the international market.

Before proceeding to a typology of the relationships between local music and national markets, a few comments should be made concerning the data used to assign cases to specific categories, as well as regarding the scope of the argument presented here. The information used to assess the specific condition of each individual country consists of music-industry statistics on the development of phonogram market size and market structure for those countries considered significant markets within the international music industry. This information possesses two weaknesses which, while they do not undermine its usefulness, nevertheless warrant comment. Firstly, this data refers to the market for phonograms (musical recordings) and does not include revenues generated through the music industry's exploitation of rights. As a result, this information does not provide an exhaustive picture of the size and structure of a given music market. The importance of rights exploitation within the music business is rapidly increasing. One indicator of this development is the growing involvement of record companies in music publishing. Only a small part of the time spent on musical consumption consists of that devoted to listening to tapes, CDs and albums bought in the shops by consumers, the traditional source of revenue for the music industry. An important objective of the music industry is that of acquiring a greater share of revenues from music which is 'freely' consumed by people, as they listen to the radio, watch television, and so on. In addition, the use of music in advertisements, motion pictures and television series offers another domain in which considerable revenues are generated for the music industry (Frith, 1988a).[3] There is, however, no indication that the revenue generated through rights exploitation is gained from types of music significantly different from those which feature prominently within the phonogram market. In this respect, the size and structure of different phonogram markets may still be used to generate valid indicators of the position of local musics.

The second weakness of the information used here lies in the fact that it is derived from those countries and territories which are considered relevant markets for the international music industry. Other countries are not included in the official marketing policy of the internationally organized industry and are, therefore, left out of the statistics. These countries are not integrated within the international music-industry system because their local infrastructures of music production and distribution do not permit that industry to operate successfully. This is a result both of the smallness of these phonogram markets relative to those of the West,[4] and of the fact that the international music industry cannot get a hold of the biggest part of these markets, due to the large share thereof taken up by pirated cassettes. Moreover, local scenes in non-Western countries are often based on other modes of production and distribution than those typical within Western countries. Live performances, for instance, seem to involve less an extension

Table 2. Four types of countries based on size of phonogram market and share of local music on the local market in 1989 and the importance of local sounds internationally

Country	Size of phon. market in US $1,000,000	Share of local music in local market in %	Importance of local sounds internationally
Type 1			
USA	6,464	69	important
UK	1,981	61	important
Type 2			
Japan	3,087	74	unimportant
France	1,325	45	unimportant
Type 3			
Italy	447	39	unimportant
Brazil	371	66	unimportant
Type 4			
Canada	594	9	unimportant
Netherlands	439	13	unimportant
Norway	104	21	unimportant

Source: Hung and Morencos (1990) and music industry sources.

of that music which is marketed and distributed by the music industry than a mode of music distribution in its own right. The analysis put forward in this article applies principally to those countries wherein the viability of local musical activity is heavily dependent on the distribution and marketing of phonograms through the structures of the music industry.

Together, the three aforementioned parameters provide a valid indicator of the economic viability of specific local sounds within existing structures for the production and distribution of music. On the basis of these parameters, a simple typology and categorization of countries and their local music may be elaborated. For convenience, only two categories indicating size, share and role will be used: big and small. Using more sophisticated measures would automatically lead to a more sophisticated typology. Furthermore, only those types for which concrete examples exist will be mentioned. This means that only four out of the hypothetical eight (2 x 2 x 2) will be discussed.

The four types which can be distinguished are:

1. A country with a big phonogram market, with a big share for local music within the turnover of the local market and a relatively important role for its local sounds within the international music market.
2. A country with a big phonogram market, with a big share for local music within the turnover of the local phonogram market and a relatively unimportant role for local sounds within the international music market.
3. A country with a small phonogram market, with a big share for local

music within the turnover of the local phonogram market and a relatively small, unimportant role for local sounds within the international music market.
4 A country with a small phonogram market, with a small share for local music within the turnover of the local phonogram market and a relatively unimportant role for local sounds within the international music market.

In Table 2, some nine countries are categorized according to the above typology. The only country which really fits the description of Type 1 completely is the United States of America. It has by far the biggest national market, and a share for local music within the national market which exceeds two-thirds. Furthermore, the US may be considered a global trendsetter as far as popular music is concerned. This holds true as well, although to a lesser extent, for the United Kingdom. The UK market is only one-third the size of the American. However, the role of British popular music within the world's overall 'sound' today is comparable to that of the US. It is clear that the structural parameters are the most favourable for both these Type 1 countries. They provide the sounds defining the world beat of today. Considering that the USA and UK are the only two countries whose music plays an important role within the structure of the international market, we may move to consider the other two parameters in this typology: those having to do with size of the market and the share of local music within the national market. This leads, first of all, to Type 2. The only country which really fits this description is Japan. To some extent France meets these criteria, as well, but the French market, like the British, should be considered as medium-sized. Also, the share of local sounds within the French market is three-fifths that of Japanese music within the Japanese market.

Two countries meeting the criteria for Type 3 are Brazil and Italy. The markets of both countries are relatively small. The share of local music within the national market is reasonable, particularly insofar as Brazil is concerned. A great many countries in the world – for example Canada, the Netherlands and Norway – meet the criteria for inclusion in Type 4.

It should be clear that a certain ranking is implicit in the typology just presented. The present condition of the international music scene works to the benefit of local musics from the United States and Great Britain, while things seem less promising for musics from the Netherlands, Canada and Norway. There are relatively large markets for American and British music within their respective home countries, as well as plenty of opportunities for this music to be marketed internationally, in large measure as a result of the cultural history of the world's popular music. The international potential of local sounds from Canada, Norway and the Netherlands is far less, given the shares they occupy within their domestic markets. The fact that there is a very limited domestic market for local musics in Type 4 countries poses important problems, given the skyrocketing costs of recording and marketing. It is necessary to look to larger markets in order to recoup investments in a band or an artist. This is highly problematic for performers from countries with small markets and small shares for local product within those markets, as these have no tradition as musical trendsetters and, consequently, little chance to market their musics abroad.

In the end, this process can lead to the withering away of a vital cultural practice, in that a whole sector of cultural activity – one consisting of musicians playing music, performing live in concert, being recorded by a local music industry and receiving airplay on domestic radio – is slowly disappearing. This is only because this activity cannot survive in a context in which the economic scale necessary for its success has been expanded beyond its own capabilities.

In more analytic terms, the typology just presented may serve as a point of departure for research into the music industry in countries which are tied in to the international music-industry system. The position of a country and its local music, within the force field outlined here, is a significant determinant of the central concerns, goals and appropriate modes of operation of the music industry within a given context. This may be illustrated with material from a study of the position of Dutch rock music within the national and international markets.

A central tension running through every segment of the Dutch music industry – be it big or small, major or independent – is that between the exploitation of national repertory (music made and recorded by Dutch artists) and that of international repertory. Most of the companies active within the Dutch market combine the exploitation of Dutch local musics with that of musics from abroad. They acquire musics of foreign origin, either through licensing deals with foreign labels (this applies to independent companies as well as majors), or by being part of a major company with a big international network through which they acquire the artists signed by sister companies in other territories. In almost every case, the greatest part of turnover and profit within the national market comes from international repertory, with the exception of one or two companies which concentrate on national musics. As previously mentioned, the Dutch office of the American Warner Music decided some time ago to end its involvement with local repertory and to serve only as the local sales office for music from abroad, primarily from the United States. Warner's principal argument was that the exploitation of local music was so time-consuming, costly and unprofitable that it prevented them from releasing commercially interesting, but less costly, material from the United States.

Let us now take a look at the way in which the national-international tension is reproduced within the operations of major companies in the Netherlands. All the major companies (Sony, Warner Music, EMI, BMG, Polygram) have offices in the Netherlands. Most of these have international headquarters in London and New York. Both the American and English units of the major companies operate almost autonomously within the structure of the majors, given that both these countries are the most important sources for new internationally marketable musics, as in Type 1 of our model. These units generate a good deal of music which offices in territories other than the US and the UK are more or less obliged to release in line with international corporate policy. The local offices of majors, like those in the Netherlands, mostly have their own A&R managers and release local product. Their most important priority with their own releases is that of recouping investments within the local market, which is increasingly difficult given the declining market share of local product within local (small) markets on the one hand, and the rising costs of recording and marketing on the other. International exploitation through affiliates abroad could offer a solution to this, but this, in most cases, is hardly possible. Local offices must fight, within the structures of their own companies, in order to have products released abroad.

Let's take the average president of the national office of a major company operating in the Netherlands. For him (it is almost always a man) it is almost impossible to get his artists released in the USA and the UK. The affiliates in those countries put out so much product themselves – product which he, along with his colleagues on the European continent, must release – that there is little room left for the exploitation of Dutch material in the UK and the US. Even if our president of the Dutch office gets the UK and the US A&R managers to listen to his artists, they easily find reasons for backing off from them. If the music sounds different from what is current in the US or UK market, they will say: 'This is not suitable for our market'. If, in contrast, it sounds English or American, the argument will take a different tack: 'We have dozens of acts like this ourselves'. So our president leaves, having accomplished nothing. Another option for our director of the Dutch office – who is very enthusiastic about his product and wants to go for international success – is to disregard the UK and the US, buy a round-trip airline ticket and visit every affiliated office on the European continent (and, maybe, Japan). He probably will get his product out in some countries, but under his arm, when he comes back, will be five to ten mastertapes of albums by acts from Italy, Spain and perhaps even Japan – albums he must release in Holland in exchange for the release of his product in those countries. Then, trying to be smart, he will release those records, send a confirmation copy to his faraway affiliates and do nothing with respect to those releases – no promotion, no plugging, etc. What he forgets, of course, is that his Italian, Spanish and Japanese colleagues are also smart (perhaps, in fact, that's why they ended up in the same business, maybe even in the same company), and they will likewise do nothing to make the release of his record a successful one. In the end, nothing happens. The local president's only success comes in being able to state, in the press release which accompanies the release of the album, that the record is out in more than ten countries around the world.

Cognizant of this way of proceeding, the directors of several affiliates of the major companies have in each case established and taken seats on European boards which attempt to agree on a list of European priorities to which each Continental office of the appropriate major may commit itself. This commitment implies a release for a record, as well as the devotion of considerable effort towards marketing and promoting it. As a result, every national office of that multinational firm attempts to get its artists on the priority list. One of the strongest arguments for being on such a list, of course, is success within the home market. If pan-European success follows, the company which signed the act has cause to once again knock on the doors of the American and British A&R managers. In many cases, the answer, even then, is 'no'.

One conclusion which might be drawn from this is that, in order to understand the workings of the music industry, and the consequences of these workings for the state of musical diversity in the world – because, in the end, this is what is at stake – one needs an approach attentive to the specific situation of each country within the world music market. This situation may be analyzed using the parameters sketched out in the course of this essay. Having determined the specific situation of each country which interests us, we must grasp those structural factors which shape the context within which the music industry operates. Doing so might require some understanding of local musical history, or grasping the legal context within which the music industry operates. Up to this point, we have been mainly concerned with contextual information, and this stage in our research is more or less in line with the so-called 'production of culture' perspective (Peterson, 1976a). A subsequent step would investigate the ways in which music-industry executives elaborate their specific forms of conduct within the contexts in which they operate. This analysis would not presume, as its point of departure, that industry policy is completely determined by these contexts, but would look at ways in which that policy results from the particular construction of realities undertaken by specific persons within specific positions within these contexts. What is needed, at this stage of research into the music industry, is an 'interpretative approach to the production of culture' (Jensen, 1984). It is precisely within that space wherein music executives construct their versions of reality that one may locate the potential for change. As Line Grenier has argued, music should be considered as essentially 'the result of a constant process of iteration between various actors who, through their respective practices, construct musics as socially and culturally meaningful realities' (Grenier, 1990: 231).

Acknowledgements

The author wishes to thank the Dutch Ministry of Culture for their support of the research on which this study is based.

Notes

1 World market is defined here as the sum of turnover in the markets of the following countries whose Music Industry Associations are members of, or affiliated to, the International Federation of the Phonographic Industry (IFPI): Argentina, Australia, Austria, Belgium, Brazil, Canada, Czechoslovakia, Denmark, Finland, France, Federal Republic of Germany, Greece, Hungary, Republic of Ireland, Italy, Japan, Netherlands, New Zealand, Norway, Portugal, Singapore, Spain, Sweden, Switzerland, United Kingdom and the United States of America.

The volume of the four markets in 1984 were (in $1,000,000): Western Europe – 2,981; United States – 4,370; Japan – 1,282; rest of the world – 1,022. In 1989, the market volumes were: Western Europe – 7,633; United States – 6,464; Japan – 3,087; rest of the world – 1,626.

The volume of the Western European market is the sum of the market volumes of the following countries: Austria, Belgium, Denmark, Finland, France, Federal Republic of Germany, Greece, Republic of Ireland, Italy, Netherlands, Portugal, Norway, Spain, Sweden, Switzerland and the United Kingdom.

2 Interview with the author, summer 1990.
3 To illustrate this point: Polygram president Alain Levy claimed in 1989 at a music industry convention held in Amsterdam that the music industry has to get between 20 and 50 per cent of its revenues out of rights exploitation in the next ten years if it wants to remain a healthy business. Russ Curry, vice-president of A&M Europe claimed: 'The music industry should stop considering itself as producers of vinyl and cardboard. We are engaged in the business of marketing of artists and their creative talent. We are right-owners.'
4 The fifteen biggest markets of the world with their turnover:

Country	Turnover in 1989 (US $1,000,000)
1 United States	6,464
2 Japan	3,087
3 United Kingdom	1,981
4 F.R.G.	1,694
5 France	1,325
6 Canada	594
7 Australia	456
8 Italy	447
9 Netherlands	439
10 Spain	431
11 Brazil	371
12 Sweden	267
13 Switzerland	214
14 Austria	176
15 Belgium	170
Others	694
Total(*)	18,810

* IFPI countries, see note 1.

Source: Hung and Morencos (1990).

References

Frith, Simon (1988a) 'Video pop: picking up the pieces', Frith (1988b): 88–130.
Frith, Simon (1988b) editor, *Facing the Music*. New York: Pantheon Books.
Grenier, Line (1990) 'Radio broadcasting in Canada: the case of "transformat" music', *Popular Music*, 9 (2) April: 221–33).

Hung, Michèle and Morencos, Esteban Garcia (1990) *World Record Sales 1969–1990, a Statistical History of the World Recording Industry*. London: International Federation of the Phonographic Industry (IFPI).
Jensen, Joli (1984) 'An interpretative approach to culture production', in Rowland *et al.* (1984): 98–118.
Peterson, Richard (1976a) 'The production of culture, a prolegomenon', in Peterson (1976b): 7–23.
Peterson, Richard (1976b) editor, *The Production of Culture*. Beverly Hills: Sage.
Rowland, W. D. *et al.* (1984) editors, *Interpreting Television*, Beverly Hills: Sage.

Paul Rutten is a communications researcher working in Holland

ROBERT WRIGHT

'GIMME SHELTER': OBSERVATIONS ON CULTURAL PROTECTIONISM AND THE RECORDING INDUSTRY IN CANADA

This paper has two related objectives. Firstly, I would like to undertake a brief review of recent Canadian policy initiatives in the areas of music broadcasting and sound recording. In particular, I shall focus on the legacy of discord which such initiatives, most notably having to do with so-called 'Canadian content', seem to have left in these industries. Secondly, and more importantly, I would like to explore the question of what we, in Canada, might reasonably expect from a policy of cultural protectionism. I want to argue that the principal objective of Canadian content legislation and of governmental involvement in the recording sector in Canada – the development of a strong indigenous recording industry – is not unrealistic, given the structure of the recording industry internationally, but has been undermined by those very policies which have sought to bring it about.

Concern for the welfare of 'Canadian culture', particularly in relation to an American mass culture, has been a central feature of national life in Canada since Confederation (1867) at least. Forms of cultural protectionism – ranging from tariffs against imported cultural goods to active support of certain cultural industries – have been a mainstay of Canadian public policy since the 1920s (Audley, 1983). In comparison with the broadcasting, magazine, book publishing and film industries – which have enjoyed the favour of legislators for much of this century – the record industry has, until quite recently, been virtually ignored by governments. This is, one may assume, because the record industry in Canada has long been regarded as both economically marginal and culturally insignificant. The question of ownership and control of the record industry in Canada did not become a matter of public discussion until the late 1960s, when an outcry on the part of such industry pioneers as Walt Grealis compelled federal policy-makers to direct their attention towards it.[1]

The record industry in Canada has been dominated throughout most of its history by a handful of multinational 'major labels', companies which are themselves integrated, vertically and horizontally, into global entertainment empires.[2] The Canadian role in this transnational record industry – one which is hardly unique within the international context – has thus been to serve as a market for mostly non-Canadian recordings of non-Canadian musical performances.[3] In part as a result of Canada's relatively high tariff on imported recordings, all of the 'majors' established subsidiary operations in Canada, where they have virtually monopolized the market (and where they continue to account for roughly 90 per cent of industry revenues). These subsidiaries are concentrated in Toronto, with a limited number of adjunct offices in other Canadian cities, and they are primarily in the business of pressing records, tapes and CDs for domestic consumption, using foreign, usually American or British, mastertapes. The subsidiaries operate with some independence, signing and promoting local talent, but this is a relatively new development and their increasingly distant relationship with their parent companies has proven to be something of a mixed blessing for Canadian recording artists. Historically, Canadian artists – from Hank Snow in the 1930s to Neil Young in the 1960s – have had little choice but to leave Canada if they hoped to have a musical career that included a record contract.

The project of mobilizing Canadian policy-makers in support of an indigenous record industry was shaped in the late 1960s by a growing public taste for music about Canada – most notably for the music of Gordon Lightfoot – and, indeed, by a growing sense of embarrassment over the fact that Canadian recording artists had to exile themselves to pursue their craft. Private radio broadcasters were singled out as having collaborated in the colonization of the Canadian recording industry, on the grounds that they had refused to sacrifice audience share (and hence advertising revenues) in order to promote Canadian artists. Responding to a growing public concern, the federal government instituted what it called 'Canadian content' legislation, to be administered by the Canadian Radio-Television and Telecommunications Commission (CRTC). Since January 1971, AM radio stations in Canada have been required to play a minimum of 30 per cent 'Cancon' as a condition of the renewal of their broadcasting licenses. Musical selections considered 'Canadian content' are those which meet two of the following criteria: (a) the instrumentation or lyrics were principally performed by a Canadian; (b) the music was performed by a Canadian; (c) the lyrics were written by a Canadian; (d) the live performance was wholly recorded in Canada. (*Record*, 1990a) The percentage of mandatory Canadian content within the playlists of FM stations was defined with specific reference to each station's programming format and audience, though it appears that recent proposals to standardize these requirements across all stations on the FM band are being seriously considered by the CRTC.

It was not until the early 1980s that the Canadian government arranged for the provision of direct subsidies to the sound-recording industry, several years after it had initiated financial support of the book-publishing and film industries. The institutional structure through which this support was channelled took the form of a private-sector agency, the Foundation to Assist Canadian Talent on Record. FACTOR was created in 1982 by several Canadian-owned private broadcasting corporations, the Canadian Independent Record Producers Association (CIRPA) and the Canadian Music Publishers Association (CMPA). It was designed to 'stimulate the growth and development of the independent sector of the Canadian recording industry' by making grants and interest-free loans available to Canadian acts on a competitive basis for the production of demos and videoclips and for the organization of international tours (FACTOR, no date).

Publicly, broadcasters expressed their desire to support the Canadian recording industry in altruistic terms, while simultaneously reasoning that if they failed to cooperate they might run the risk of having too little Canadian product for their playlists. Under the terms of the 1970 Cancon legislation, however, private broadcasters are required not only to play Canadian music but to actively promote Canadian talent off-air (although the CRTC has never specified the proportion of profit each station is expected to spend on this promotion). To be sure, membership in FACTOR has not gone unnoticed by the CRTC in its consideration of broadcast license renewal applications.

With FACTOR in place but woefully underfunded – its first annual budget was $200,000 (Canadian), too little to capitalize the production of more than two record albums – the federal government announced the creation in 1986 of a Sound Recording Development Program (SRDP), which would pump $25 million into the Canadian recording industry over five years. The SRDP includes three major components – production support ($18 million), promotion, touring and marketing support ($4.5 million), and business development ($2.5 million). FACTOR and its French-language counterpart (MUSICACTION), which was founded in 1985, receive $2.2 million annually from SRDP funds. This amount, along with an increased commitment from the private sector, has brought FACTOR's annual operating budget to roughly $4 million in 1990. The rationale for government involvement in the FACTOR program, as expressed in *Vital Links*, an influential booklet published by the Department of Communications, was that the

> recent serious decline in the number of Canadian content recordings – especially the precipitous 45 per cent drop in French-language production since 1978 – had created problems for Canada's radio broadcasters, who are finding it difficult to obtain an adequate supply of new releases. (Department of Communications, 1987: 54)

Support for the indigenous recording industry continues to make good nationalist fodder, however; at the press conference announcing the SRDP, held at a Montreal disco, Communications Minister Marcel Masse was quoted as saying that 'the sorry state of Canada's recording industry is due to the viselike control exercised by multinational companies over the distribution of records in Canada' (*Global and Mail*, 1986). In November of 1991, at the end of SRDP's first five years of operation, the Federal government announced that it had become a permanent program, with an annual budget of $5 million.

Since their inception, Canadian content legislation and, to a lesser extent, FACTOR itself have been subject to controversy within the recording and broadcasting sectors, as well as among policy-makers and outside observers. At the level of the industries themselves, support for Cancon has tended to coalesce around the Canadian Independent Record Producers Association, while opposition has emanated most noticeably from the Canadian Association of Broadcasters (CAB).

CIRPA was founded in 1975 as a voluntary association for Canada's independent record companies (of which there are now estimated to be about 130), and has assumed the crucial role of watchdog and lobbyist for the independent Canadian record industry. CIRPA's position on Canadian content is unequivocal: it sees the very survival of the Canadian recording industry as hinging on radio exposure for Canadian acts. Thus, the Association is presently lobbying not only for increased Canadian-content requirements for FM radio – which, it argues, will represent simply a return to the 'status quo ante of 1971, when AM was the band of choice' – but for a much more strenuous monitoring policy that will prevent broadcasters from playing their requisite Canadian content in non-peak periods.[4] CIRPA's position is supported tacitly by the influential Canadian record industry trade paper *The Record* (see Farrell, 1990) and explicitly by several of the country's most influential rock music critics, most notably Chris Dafoe of the Toronto daily newspaper the *Star*. Remarkable for its absence in the debate over Cancon is the Canadian Recording Industry Association (CRIA), which represents the major label subsidiaries in Canada and for which, therefore, the country of origin of recorded 'product' is of far less importance than its overall sales in the Canadian market.

The positions of the CAB, the association representing private broadcasters in Canada, are explicitly opposed to those of CIRPA. Given that the CAB speaks exclusively for the interests of private-sector capital, it is not easy to distil specific objections to Cancon from the Association's generalized resentment of regulation of its industry. The broad outlines of its case are, however, clear. A CAB survey of FM radio programmers conducted in 1990 revealed that very few broadcasters believe there is 'enough Canadian music to sustain a higher quota.' In a moment of rare candour, radio entrepreneur Bill Gilliland – with the sponsorship of 'concerned music industryites' – articulated in *The Record* what is undoubtedly a widely held view of the Canadian record industry among broadcasters:

> Throughout the '60s and '70s and '80s, radio programmers across Canada busted their buns devising creative and effective ways to present the nation's music artists to listeners. Beginning in the mid-'80s, music

video programmers added their very, very substantial support to the record industry by imaginatively presenting the nation's music artists to viewers. Radio and video support continues in the '90s. Why, then, aren't the made-in-Canada recording artists as successful as many critics think they should be? Is the market for domestic recording artists grossly overestimated? (Quoted in *Record*, 1990d)

Implicit in Gilliland's observations is the suggestion that some radio programmers in Canada have reservations, not only about the quantity of Canadian musical recordings, but about their quality as well.

At the level of policy analysis, traditionally the domain of economists and academic observers, the debate over Canadian content has tended to centre on the more generalized question of its value – or even its utility – for Canadians and for 'Canadian culture'. Unlike the debate between independent recording companies and radio interests, this is a debate about first principles. For Paul Audley, one of several independent policy analysts whose writing echoes the official governmental line about Cancon, any discussion of the subject must begin with the premise that 'Canadians who are involved in the creation and performance of music ought to have a fair chance to have their music recorded and played on radio stations in Canada' (Audley, 1983: 139). This position has been restated as recently as November 1990 by CRTC policy analyst John Feihl, who would urge us to 'change our perspective' on the Cancon issue by asking not whether 30 per cent Cancon is too much, but whether 70 per cent non-Canadian content is too little (Feihl, 1990: 32).

The widespread consensus in favour of Canadian-content regulations, outside of certain narrowly partisan circles, is evident in the low number of policy analysts who have criticized the assumptions upon which it rests. I am aware of only one recent scholarly work, William Watson's *National Pastimes: The Economics of Canadian Leisure* (1988) that comes out squarely in favour of dismantling Canadian-content policy as it is presently constituted, and my suspicion is that because this work has been published by a conservative, free-market-oriented think-tank – the Fraser Institute – it is unlikely to get a fair hearing. Watson's methodology is simple, perhaps deceptively so: as an economist, he wants to ask whether Canadians get their money's worth, quite literally, from Canadian-content regulations. Most of the leisure goods consumed within Canada, he observes, are not subsidized, while most of those which may be designated Canadian-content receive some form of subsidy. Watson asks whether a performer or a recording may be said to provide benefits to the people who have paid for it via their taxes, but who have not seen or heard it because it was of too little value to do so. With regard to sound recordings, Watson argues that, at most, we should be subsidizing activities that teach Canadians about each other, and that the pertinent criteria for eligibility as Canadian content should therefore be the 'Canadianness' of a recording's subject matter rather than of its production. He asks: 'Should the [Canadian] state really have a position on where the generic rock music Canadians listen to is produced?' The answer: '[S]ound-alike recordings by such people as Corey Hart, Bryan Adams and Luba, [which are] destined for the US market have no claim to public support' (Watson, 1988: 112).

Regardless of one's ideological proximity to Watson, his insistence that Canadian tax-payers/consumers themselves be brought into the debate is a challenge that cannot be lightly dismissed. Indeed, taken alongside charges made by the Canadian Association of Broadcasters – to the effect that radio audience shares decrease in direct proportion to the amount of Canadian content broadcast – there is a certain force to the argument that so-called ordinary Canadians cast their votes on Canadian content with their ears, i.e., with their radio tuners and record-buying dollars.

If conservative critics of Cancon, like William Watson and the CAB, were alone in advancing the argument that the consumption of recorded music ought to be driven by 'market forces', the suggestion that Canadians vote with their ears might be easily dismissed. The truth of the matter is that even ardent Cancon supporters acknowledge that the main preoccupation of the Canadian music industry – and therefore of the CRTC and FACTOR – is not one of protecting or enhancing 'Canadian culture' so much as it is that of finding and developing *international* markets.

Canadian-content requirements, as envisaged by the CRTC, have been driven by two main goals: the development of a Canadian recording industry and the nurturing and support of Canadian musical talent. However compatible these objectives might seem as matters of policy, in practice they have proven to be at odds. Because of the dominant position of the major multinational labels both domestically and internationally, Canadian recording artists have always recognized that their greatest success is likely to come in the form of an international record contract. This is as true for the 1990s as it was for the 1930s – the top-selling Canadian acts have always been those which produce records for major foreign record companies. In 1984, a celebrated but by no means exceptional year within the recent history of the Canadian recording industry, the top-selling Canadian rock acts – Bryan Adams, Helix, Platinum Blonde, Corey Hart and Honeymoon Suite – were all signed to major multinational record deals and actually broke first in the United States (Quill, 1984).

What is more, the success – and even the survival – of independent Canadian record companies is tied to their ability to expand their markets beyond Canada. The reason for this, simply stated, is that the Canadian market for records is too small in all but a handful of cases to recover the costs of production: an album has to go Gold (50,000 copies in Canada) before the costs of bringing a new act onstream – including recording, marketing, touring and videos – (usually estimated to lie between $100,000 and $250,000) are likely to be recovered. Thus, the most successful Canadian independent labels (unaffiliated with transnational firms) are: those which distribute foreign product in Canada – as in the case of Attic Records; those which have managed to crack international markets with Canadian product – notably Nettwerk and True North; or, most ironically of all, those which have managed to break non-Canadian performers in international markets – Stony Plain, for example. (See, for example, Lacey, 1986).

Thus, to be a successful Canadian recording artist or Canadian record company is, paradoxically, to have broken into international markets. Consequently, the most successful Canadian musicians and record companies are those which fit most readily into the larger world of Anglo-American popular music. This has long been the rule of thumb for musicians and record-company executives in Canada; it is now the guiding principle of Ottawa's policy on the subsidization of the recording industry. As *Vital Links* put it in 1987:

> In most cases, export sales are ... essential if Canadian-owned companies are to turn a profit on a recording project. Efforts must be made, therefore, to tour the artist internationally and to license Canadian products to recording and music-publishing companies in other countries. (Department of Communications, 1987: 1953)

To this end, it was decided in October 1990 that FACTOR funding for Canadian recording projects would be 'earmarked for fewer artists in order to deliver product better suited for the international market', with the result that 'individual labels would of necessity be eligible for fewer projects' (Bateman, 1990). CIRPA followed suit in 1990, presenting a report to the Ontario Ministry of Culture and Communications requesting $5 million-per-annum for, among other things, 'assistance in expanding foreign markets' (*Record*, 1990e).

Since the objectives of the CRTC are those of strengthening the recording industry in Canada and supporting Canadian acts, the success of Canadian-content legislation should be judged in part in terms of its success in carrying Canadian musicians and Canadian product into foreign markets. When so judged, as virtually everyone in the broadcasting and recording industries seems to agree, Cancon is found wanting. As one Canadian record executive stated bluntly in 1980:

> So much garbage was being recorded just to help fill the airways that a lot of third-rate stuff was called a hit. What was worse came when you took a *good* record that was a Canadian hit to the States. They wouldn't listen. To them, a Canadian hit meant second-rate. (Quoted in Goddard, 1980)

It is not only performers signed to independent Canadian labels which suffer this fate. On the contrary, as Toronto singer/songwriter Andrew Cash noted in 1986, the multinationals are even suspicious of the judgements of their Canadian branches:

> Most Canadian record companies are US-owned subsidiaries and many of the local acts they've signed – Gowan, New Regime, Parachute Club – haven't been picked up in the US. What's the point in pinning your hopes on a big contract and allowing yourself to be moulded and processed if

you end up getting dropped after one or two records, just because the US parent company wasn't interested . . .? (Quoted in Quill, 1986)

Rather than stimulating exposure for Canadian product in non-Canadian markets, Cancon has contributed to the perception, however valid, that this product is inferior. As veteran Canadian rock critic Peter Goddard suggested in 1980:

> Ironically, the legislated Canadian content regulations . . . undermined [the] international impact [of Canadian acts]. Soon enough, artists who had the clout – from Anne Murray and Gordon Lightfoot to most recently Martha and the Muffins and the Sharks – signed with either British or American companies; hits outside Canada were the name of the game. (Goddard, 1980)

Fellow critic Craig MacInnis (1987) has called this 'the sure-it's-a-gold-record-in-Canada-but-will-it-play-in-Boise syndrome'.

The central paradox of cultural protectionism in the recording industry – and this applies to both Cancon legislation and direct subsidization of sound recordings – is that the criteria by which Canadian acts qualify for support is their appeal in international markets. 'Distinctive' Canadian recordings do not necessarily qualify since they are unlikely to make the tight playlists of commercial radio and are unlikely to sell well internationally. Thus, to echo William Watson, the argument can be made that Canadian-content legislation and government subsidization of the recording industry, rather than preserving whatever is distinctive about Canadian culture or teaching Canadians about each other, are effectively homogenizing Canadian musical culture along lines dictated by the multinational Anglo-American recording industry. As Goddard (1980) puts it, 'No one at the centres of pop power in New York or Los Angeles gives a gilt-edged hoot about regional sound or style unless it can move 50,000 units a day.'

Nowhere is this paradox more strikingly evident than in the designation of Canadian-content recordings for radio airplay. Non-Canadian acts covering domestic copyrights qualify as Cancon – recent examples of this phenomenon include the Neville Brothers' cover of Leonard Cohen's 'Bird On A Wire' and Aerosmith's 'The Other Side'. As Laura Bartlett, Promotion V-P of Virgin Canada, noted in July 1990:

> A situation such as Aerosmith is completely absurd. If I phone my Los Angeles office and tell them that Colin James [a Canadian blues-rock performer] (lacking in sufficient Cancon points) is not Canadian content but Aerosmith is, they'll think I lost my mind. (Quoted in *Record*, 1990b)

Moreover, a Canadian artist living in Canada and paying taxes here who goes to the United States and records an American song – as in the case, for example, of recent material from Colin James, k. d. lang, Lori Yates and others – fails to qualify for Cancon certification. Since it is axiomatic that private broadcasters will play only the minimum level of Canadian content, Canadians' failure to meet Cancon regulations has the effect of actually shutting them out of their home market. The situation has grown so bad that BMG Canada has adopted a policy of re-recording non-Cancon tracks by Canadian artists in Canada so as to meet the terms of Canadian-content eligibility. Michelle Wright and Jeff Healey are two artists distributed by BMG who re-recorded tracks in Canada using Canadian musicians. As CBS national-promotion director Shan Kelly has stated bluntly: '[O]verall, I believe that Cancon ghettoizes Canadian music' (*Record*, 1990c).

I am less interested in the question of whether there is anything worth preserving in Canadian musical culture than in the pragmatic question of what, in the last analysis, we might reasonably expect from a policy of cultural protectionism. Since Canadian-content legislation and direct subsidization of the record industry have neither produced a strong recording industry nor affected musicians' aspirations, I think it fair to ask whether the nationalist vision that informed such policies – to produce made-in-Canada stars who achieve international success while remaining on a Canadian label – were ever viable. I would argue not only that this objective was unreasonable but that, in truth, the pragmatic business of accommodating to the dominant agenda of the multinational music industry has worked against such a vision.

Cancon regulations and the subsidization of the recording industry could never have produced a competitive Canadian recording industry because at a pragmatic level these mechanisms have evolved into means of improving Canadian musicians' chances in a global industry dominated by the multinationals. Cultural protectionism may allow – or force – Canadians to hear more music by Canadian artists on the radio, and it may stimulate interest for this recorded product nationally. However, no interventionist policy will enable Canadian record companies to compete with the multinationals internationally; on the contrary, there is strong evidence to suggest that official protectionism has limited the ability of indigenous companies and artists to compete outside Canada.

My argument is not that these protectionist policies are poorly conceived or even that they have failed in practice, but rather that they have been found inadequate when measured against the nationalist agenda out of which they arose in the 1970s and against which they continue to be measured. Cancon legislation has failed to serve as a launching pad from which Canadian performers might attain international stardom, and this failure was inevitable. The most we might have asked of it is that it help the Blue Rodeos and the Parachute Clubs to a portion of the Canadian market. The worst we might have feared is that it would ghettoize such acts and so reduce their chances of international success.

Similarly, the most that we might ask from programs like FACTOR and the SRDP is that they will continue to assist independent record production in Canada. The key term here is not 'Canada', however, but 'independent', for it is the nature of independent labels – whether in Canada or elsewhere – to play an adjunct role in a world dominated by the majors. Independent labels bear the lion's share of responsibility for seeking out and nurturing new talent, knowing full well that, once discovered, this talent is likely to be appropriated by a major label. Cultural protectionism could never have been expected to increase the Canadian indies' share of the international market but what it has done – and this point should be underscored – is to broaden dramatically the volume and range of Canadian recorded product available to Canadian consumers. If all that such institutions as FACTOR ever accomplish is keeping Canadian indies afloat – as a source of Canadian music for Canadian consumers, but also as a source of a new talent for world markets – they will have succeeded admirably.

Notes

1 Walt Grealis was publisher of the music-industry trade magazine *RPM* which, in the early and late 1960s, was a leading nationalist voice calling for government protection of the domestic recording industry.
2 Although the relative strength and presence of these labels is slightly different in the Canadian case from that of other countries, these are the same major firms which dominate the recording industry internationally at the present time: Polygram, BMG, Sony Music, Warner Music, MCA, and Capital-EMI.
3 The uniformity of this pattern is outlined at length in Wallis and Malm (1984).
4 'Executive Directors' report', *CIRPA Newsletter*, August 1990, p. 1. See also Farrell (1990). CIRPA is also leading the campaign for more rigorous copyright legislation in Canada.

References

Audley, Paul (1983) *Canada's Cultural Industries: Broadcasting, Publishing, Records and Film*. Toronto: Lorimer.
Bateman, Jeff (1990) 'FACTOR vetting quality over quantity', *The Record*, 8 October, 1990.
Department of Communications (1987) *Vital Links: Canadian Cultural Industries*. Ottawa: Government of Canada, Department of Communications.
FACTOR [The Foundation to Assist Canadian Talent on Record) (no date) Untitled pamphlet.
Farrell, David (1990) 'FM regs help promote fool's gold', *The Record*, 6 August 1990.
Feihl, John (1990) 'The impact of the Canadian content regulations on the Canadian recording industry', *Association of Canadian Studies Newsletter* 12 (3) (Fall, 1990): 32.
Goddard, Peter (1980) 'Pop record makers ignore borders', *Toronto Star*, 15 November 1980.
Globe and Mail (1986) 'Ottawa to help record industry change its tune', 10 May 1986.
Lacey, Liam (1986) 'Little labels can make a big mark', *Globe and Mail*, 4 April 1986.
MacInnis, Craig (1987) 'High price of selling rock', *Toronto Star*, 29 December 1987.
Quill, Greg (1984) 'Record industry needs new deal', *Toronto Star*, 1 December 1984.
—— (1986) 'What *do* most indies want?', *Toronto Star*, 21 February 1986.
Record, The (1990a) 'CRTC guidelines', 23 July 1990.
—— (1990b) 'Cancon reg has industry seeing red', 23 July 1990.
—— (1990c) 'Canadian artists resort to re-recording songs', 23 July 1990.
—— (1990d) 'Gilliland proposes 30% music content for daily newspapers and consumer magazines', 13 August 1990.

—— (1990e) 'CIRPA study recommends Ontario support program', 15 October 1990.
Wallis, Roger and Malm, Krister (1984) *Big Sounds From Small People: The Music Industry in Small Countries*. New York: Pendragon.
Watson, William (1988) *National Pastimes: The Economics of Canadian Leisure* Vancouver: The Fraser Institute.

Robert Wright teaches History and Cultural Studies at Trent University in Peterborough, Canada

JODY BERLAND

FREE TRADE AND CANADIAN MUSIC: LEVEL PLAYING FIELD OR SCORCHED EARTH?

Canadians live with an endemic, popular and (until recently) officially sanctioned awareness and resentment of multinational corporate dominance that has pervaded their public culture for many decades. Since Canada's origin as a nation-state, this public culture has relied on political, legal and symbolic discourses that represented its culture, media, and identity as fragile subjects of external domination and colonization. Yet this resentment has never been lastingly attached to any singular or unified culture as its perceived victim. Perhaps this is because colonization through domination of communication media is an older problem for Canada than for most other constituencies now enjoying its effects, while the country itself is relatively new in relation to the sweep of Western colonization across the world. Aside from aboriginal cultures, Canada possesses no originary identity independent of such colonization.

In a time when controversies about local, national and international cultural identities, movements and economies have moved to the forefront of political and academic discussion, Canada's situation is therefore both exemplary and anomalous. In Canada, the cultural and economic problems accompanying nationalization-denationalization-internationalization of the media have been very visible where they are elsewhere more latent (in terms of economic, technological and political change), and invisible where elsewhere they are more overt (in terms of impact on pre-colonial cultural forms). This structural oddity helps explain why Canada has provided the favourite example for so many scholarly discussions of electronic colonialism (e.g. Smith, 1980; Murphy, 1983).

As Kurt Blaukopf has noted: 'Canada is a particularly suitable object of comparison with such countries in Europe, since it is an industrially advanced country which in terms of cultural communication through the media is exposed to the influence of its neighbour, the USA, with its much stronger media potential.' He adds: 'A Canadian expert recently stated that the general rehearsal for the impact of new technologies on cultural communication had already taken place in Canada. That is why comparative studies throwing light on the relations between media policy, cultural policy and cultural communication in Canada and in western European countries are extremely useful.' (1987: 16)

It is not surprising then that observers of the recent Free Trade Agreement signed between Canada and the US argue that this Agreement has profound implications for changing global trade and cultural relations. The accelerating transnationalization of the media presents issues which are both economic and cultural in scope, and which force students of popular music, as of other cultural forms, to reflect in new ways on the relations between economic and cultural processes and between these processes, opposing interest groups, and questions of colonization, nationalism, and national identity.

The omnipresent colonization that has simultaneously formed and de-formed Canada goes some distance to explaining why it seems so difficult to address such issues, currently exemplified by the corporate and political developments effected by the Free Trade Agreement, as they may affect music, the industry, the economy, or any other subject, without appearing to be riddled with regressive nationalism and thus incapable of conceptualizing the real significance of the new era. What follows is, among other things, a preliminary exploration of this problematic.

I will begin by summarizing the background and social physiognomy of the Free Trade Agreement dispute as it relates to the culture industries. I will then discuss some of its general ramifications and consider some of its possible implications for the Canadian music industry.

Free trade: from 'scorched earth' to 'level playing field'?

The first initiatives for negotiating a special freer trade agreement between Canada and the US came from American trade officials in 1983 as part of a planned new round of world trade talks. According to research published by Joyce Nelson, such initiatives were in large part a response to new and proposed trade restrictions on America's fastest growing corporate conglomerate: the entertainment industries. The US Ambassador chose Canada as its first prospect for new trade talks during a time when all of its major trading partners were building protective walls. One such threat came from Quebec, Canada's most nationalist province, whose Fournier Commission proposed a new Cinema Law in 1982 that would repatriate film distribution in favour of indigenous film distribution and subsidized local production. In supporting the Bill, PQ Culture Minister Clement Richard stated that 'To consider only the laws of the market and, in addition, to promote that option, would mean to turn over Quebec's cinema industry to the American majors, bound hand and foot. This would be tantamount to assassinating Quebec's entire cinema industry.' (Nelson, 1986: 18)

For Richard, as for most Canadians, that all-important notion of fair play meant something quite different from the 'level playing field' later evoked by Canada's Conservative government to describe free trade. In a series of political manoeuvres familiar to observers of Canadian film-industry history, the Quebec Bill was opposed by the Motion Pictures Association of America (MPAA) and its Canadian representatives, who equated Quebec with Mozambique and threatened a major boycott of Quebec screens (backed by a letter from the US consulate mentioning 'possible countermeasures') should the Bill be passed. The use of the term 'scorched earth' to describe such threats was by 1985 a central feature of the tactical rhetoric of American corporations such as Gulf and Western, who were engaged in a similar political battle over legislation prohibiting American acquisitions of Canadian publishing companies. Gulf and Western's Washington lobbyist contacted Canadian Ambassador Gotlieb and, according to a 1985 *Toronto Star* article, 'warned him that unless the Canadian government toed the line, Gulf and Western would adopt' a 'scorched-earth policy' – 'presumably the patriation of Prentice-Hall to the United States with a consequent loss of many jobs and also perhaps some nasty moves in the Canadian film industry' (Cahill, 1985: B1).

By 1985, the Free Trade Agreement was the subject of a full-scale media battle; newspaper headlines warned: 'Threat to culture seen: free trade with US could destroy cultural industries' (*Winnipeg Free Press*, 23 December, 1985); 'Canadian culture seen as pawn in free trade talks' (*Toronto Star*, 2 August 1986); 'Battle lines drawn for cabinet battle over cultural future'; 'Politicians set for fierce fight over culture' (*Toronto Star*, 5 August 1986); 'Canada is fighting bravely in war for cultural identity' (*Toronto Star*, 3 August 1986); and my favourite, on a nominally more humorous note: 'Free trade threatens our smuggling heritage' (*Montreal Gazette*, 12 November 1988). If Canada is subsumed into a continental economy, what happens to our longstanding habit (generally overlooked by border guards, whose welcoming indifference metonymically reminds homecoming travellers of Canada's difference from the more militaristic and zealously policed US) of smuggling bluejeans or bourbon across the border?

That this press disturbance was not simply a moral panic stirred up by a few patriotic journalists was demonstrated by widespread political opposition to the Agreement between 1985 and 1989, in the course of which national organizations representing women's organizations, public sector and trade unions, farmers and nurses, artists and actors, teachers and students, and the independent cultural industries in film, publishing and music, co-operated in the production of many research publications, benefit performances and various media events.

Where this coalition found consensus was in its opposition to the freeing of various sectors of the economy from government intervention. The opposition between the two camps was thus from the beginning structured by an antagonism between two different conceptions of the proper relation between industry and the state. Advocates of the Agreement favoured the prospective advantages to economic growth that would be created by unregulated markets within the two countries and unregulated trade between them. Opponents of this image of a 'level playing field' critically observed that the latter – unregulated trade – required the former –

unregulated markets within each country – as a precondition to the Agreement, and therefore posited the political tradition of one country as a model for the other.

This observation was not imaginary, or even contentious, since it was precisely this precondition that motivated American and Canadian business and government officials to initiate the Agreement in the first place. A 1984 US study on 'Trade barriers to US motion picture and television prerecorded entertainment, publishing and advertising industries', published under CBS chairman Thomas Wyman, identified Canada as the major offender in prohibiting US free trade, or what is more commonly known as 'free flow' of information and cultural products. This US study identified Canada ('among other countries to a lesser degree') as committing a number of 'unfair trade practices', including import quotas, restrictions on US-produced commercials, state-owned production and distribution facilities which are 'unfair competition' to private companies, foreign ownership restrictions, discriminatory tax rules, and unfair customs practices (Jephcott, 1985). The US position was that government subsidies or other interferences with free-market trade practices had to be abolished; the position of Canadian critics of the Agreement was that such abolition would lead to the elimination or radical curtailment of the independent communications/cultural industries within Canada.

Notwithstanding popular opposition to this Agreement, it was signed in late 1988 and passed into law in January 1989. Its import with respect to cultural industries is that it legalizes the concept of 'unfair competition' by permitting retaliatory measures against protectionist policies in the form of equivalent commercial penalties. In other words, a one-million dollar government subsidy to book or record production, for example, could be countered by a one-million dollar penalty (in the form of US tariffs) against Canadian exporters of wheat, timber, records, books or any other commodity. The specific protection of cultural products, practices, and traditions within a country (in this case, Canada) is thereby legally abolished as the right of government. The production and exchange of culture as pure commodity is thus enshrined in law by an international agreement that legally overrides national policies of either government (see Patrick, 1989).

For this reason, the FTA both invokes and complicates a nationalist politics, since legally, if not economically or ideologically, this provision disadvantages public policies for both countries equally. It is not (in abstract legal terms) one people and their government disadvantaged in relation to another, but government powers curtailed *per se* in relation to multinational corporate trade. Its passing has been accompanied by a visible shift in Canadian government rhetoric and in the manner in which government regulates and stimulates cultural production within the country.

Canada's Conservative government (which lost the popular vote, but won the election, on this issue) represented free trade as creating a 'level playing field' between Canada and the US in which entrepreneurs would be able to merge and expand more efficiently without protectionism or any non-economically motivated public-policy interventions (such as antimonopoly restrictions, which have also been 'liberalized'). The oddly matched terms 'level playing field' and 'scorched earth' emerged during this period as differently connotated signifiers of the inevitable progressive march towards economic continentalism. Both refer to the shift towards liberalization of the market and the retraction of government controls and subsidies; the term 'level playing field' portrays this as a benign game, and 'scorched-earth policy' warns of belligerent consequences should Canada fail to concur with this perception. Note that for Canadian spokespeople the stakes were represented as being of a ritualistic and purely economic nature, while for the Americans it was a geo-political war. Their common topographic motif draws our attention to another familiar trope: the well-known role played historically by Canada in the provision of raw materials, or staples, to a technologically and economically dominant manufacturing class in the US, which thereupon consolidated itself as imperial centre in relation to its closest and most important colony. For Innis, writing about the rise of the mass press in the US, such raw materials came in the form of trees (Innis, 1972). Now, with $1.5 billion accruing to the US annually from Canadian markets in the cultural industries, it's also markets for movies and other products of the cultural industries, and of course, turning to our present subject, musicians.

A 'cultural clearcut': free trade and the music industry

There are few clauses or provisions in the Free Trade Agreement that bear directly on the cultural industries. Despite government's insistent claims that culture was exempted from the deal in response to public pressure, its effects on the music industry will probably be substantial, especially in conjunction with other shifts in public policy and international trade. The Agreement does contain a provision to eliminate tariffs on imported film, tapes and records over the next decade, which could substantially affect manufacturing facilities within the country, and, according to some spokespeople in the music industry, shift most record manufacturing to south of the border, with obvious consequences for the Canadian music industry.

More generally, it is expected that public support for music may have to be cut back or reorganized to accord with the new level field. In fact, this internal reorientation of the music industry has been taking place since the early 1980s, most conspicuously in the form of major cutbacks to Canada's public broadcasting system, the CBC. What I want to do here is look briefly at such trends in the context of these larger shifts.

Aside from the Canadian-content quotas for radio, which were introduced in 1971 (for AM radio) and 1975 (for FM), and which did not substantially alter ownership or distribution structures in the Canadian recording industry, there was no vehicle for public support of popular music until the Department of Communications initiated the Sound Recording Development Program (SRDP) in 1985. Since the 1930s, government commissions, studies and support programs have emphasized the vulnerability of Canadian producers in film, book and periodical publishing, and broadcasting, but have tended to overlook the music industry with the covert assumption that its commercialism and dominance by multinationals made it a poor prospect for government support. The invisibility of the music industry in most policy reviews and initiatives is one reason that the effects of free trade on musicians and music production have been less prominent in the press than those on film, publishing and the wider economy.

Thus the SRDP seemed to imply a radical change in government policy on sound recording. The $25 million allocated to the Program in 1985[1] was to be administered by FACTOR, an alliance of private broadcasters already subsidizing Canadian recording (mainly targeted for MOR and other mainstream formats) as a response to the Canadian-content quotas for radio. The new fund would support recording, videos, touring and promotion, and business development in the music industry. Notable in the Program's mandate was its provision to fund international touring; musicians could receive support for tours outside the country, but not within it. This reveals how much the SRDP is in fact a negotiated response to contradictory pressures: the increasing political pressure to support Canadian independent music recording, and the increasing economic pressure to support recordings directed to the US market.

In 1985 several Canadian acts soared to the top of *Billboard* charts and many others had hits within the country. At the same time there was an increase of bankruptcies among independent labels within the country, and the French-language industry suffered a major temporary decline in recording and sales. The music press was full of statements by musicians expressing their anger and frustration at the difficulties of surviving in the Canadian music industry. By the end of 1985, Bernie Finkelstein of True North Records would note: 'Canada is not a free marketplace. Canada is basically a third world country by definition. We do not own distribution, we do not own manufacturing – which is the definition at the U.N. of a third world country . . . The sad fact is that Canada has less acts signed on a per capita basis than any other country in the world that I know of.' (*Music Scene*, January/February, 1986)

That same year – 1985 – foreign control of Canada-wide record distribution become absolute: 100 per cent. The major question being posed by musicians and composers was not how to go about exporting records to the US or elsewhere, but how to gain normal access to the Canadian record market. The SRDP was designed to change this by creating a thriving self-sufficient music business. As a result Canadian independent labels have produced a growing number of musicians achieving national acclaim. Yet, at the same time, successful promotion in the US market has been less and less related to popular or commercial success within Canada, and so success within Canada has become less important to musicians and producers as part of their economic strategy or their professional goals. In the music press, celebration of a band's success now generally refers to success in the US. For musicians, producers, and independent record companies, the goal of self-sufficiency for a national market – expressed frequently in the music press in the mid-1980s – has been rapidly overshadowed by a new pragmatic continentalism, which recognizes the rising stakes of competing in the US and international market as more and more difficult yet more and more imperative.

As a recent report for Canada's Department of Communications (DOC) argues, the rising costs of recording and video-making mean that few albums can recoup costs of production, even with SRDP loans, from domestic sales alone. 'For both artists and independent companies to survive, Canadian-originated records must now start to earn a more substantial portion of their revenues outside of Canada while Canadian-based independent record companies need to secure foreign releases or find support of foreign licensees who will import directly from Canada' (Leblanc, 1990: 31).

As a consequence more Canadian musicians now bypass Canadian companies, whose ability to function in the American market is not increased by these measures, and seek record deals with the home office of the major companies, as recent signings of artists such as Alannah Myles, Michelle Wright, k.d. lang, Jeff Healey Band and others attest. Since American companies have better access to the promotional instruments of the American (and international) industry, Canadian companies are being devalorized in terms of their contribution to the production of the music. By extension, so is the cross-country urban network of community/camps radio stations which support local music in contradistinction to the commercial stations whose formats are the explicit destination of FACTOR-funded recordings. Like the trees of the nineteenth century, Canadian resources in the form of raw talent are once again being processed for export in unmanufactured form, leaving a selective clearcut of the local industry in their wake.

Future prospects are that the global concentration of the industry will create pressures for greater government subsidy for Canadian recording (the above report for DOC being a typical example). However if such subsidy makes a significant impact on the industry or, especially, seeks to intervene in the crucial arena of distribution, the Free Trade Agreement can be invoked to prevent such repatriation. Such 'unfair trade subsidies' are increasingly fragile both economically and politically, not because they don't have popular support within the country, but because they are too expensive for a government committed to reduced public spending as befits a level playing field. In addition to this, they are now at least arguably illegal in international law. On the other hand, this doesn't necessarily make us a Third World country: as one Canadian producer and agent commented in a 1988 forum on music and free trade: 'If this were a third world country, the government would have been tried for treason for this.' (Flohill, 1988: 22).

Conclusion

I'd like to conclude by drawing out some of the connections between these developments and the problems surrounding discourses on nationalism and culture in the current period. Political developments and changes in the music industry in the 1980s produced a flurry of published opinions from the

Canadian music and recording community. Canadian composers and musicians' associations and magazines show that Canadian agents, producers, musicians and owners of independent labels have been angry and disturbed at the difficulty of working within their own national market. This doesn't mean that they don't share the aspiration of making it in the US, but rather that they want to retain their own country – still a different country with different experiences, tastes and sounds, not to mention economic institutions and ideologies – as somewhere to start and somewhere to come back to, and for some, as somewhere to stay.

Whether Canadian culture can be identified or defended as a unitary 'national subject' in this picture is of little theoretical interest to a community of musicians and cultural producers who recognize a working oppression which affects them and which they discuss, in contexts related to music-industry issues, in terms of their Canadian nationality. The point has been made often enough about women, who seek to repossess and redefine a role as speaking subjects at a time when European and postmodern theory pronounces the death of the subject (exhibiting thereby what the Femmamatics call the '"You can't fire me, I quit" syndrome' (Femmamatics, 1990)). Similarly, my own recurrent attention to the Canadian problematic is haunted by the recognition that, as Eagleton writes in his essay on nationalism and colonialism:

> All oppositional politics thus move under the sign of irony, knowing themselves ineluctably parasitic on their antagonists. Our grudge against the ruling order is not only that it has oppressed us in our social, sexual, or racial identities, but that it has thereby forced us to lavish an extraordinary amount of attention on these things, which are not in the long run all that important. (Eagleton, 1990: 26)

Of course Canadians, like the Irish of whom Eagleton writes, have not been oppressed in terms of ethnicity *per se* but rather in terms of territory, labor power, and the control of markets. It is natural to seek repossession in these terms when it is in these terms that Canadian subjects are colonized. To become autonomous as producers or as consumers of popular music, a role which such music constantly promises us, is to address that oppression and seek to come out the other side.

Note

1 According to one independent label exec speaking several months before the plan was launched, this is the amount of federal sales taxes generated by record sales. Al Mair, President of Attic Records, at the Third Annual *Record* Conference in Toronto: 'We are told that 47 per cent of all Canadian labels operate at a loss. The government assists the film and book publishing industries, yet the record business is handed less than $200,000 a year, despite the fact that record sales generate $25 million in federal sales taxes alone.' (*The Music Scene*, Jan/Feb 1986: 9.) The five-year $25 million plan was announced six months after the event.

References

Blaukopf, Kurt (1987) 'Cultural change and new technologies: the problem areas', in *Media: A Challenge to Cultural Policies*. Vienna: Mediacult VWGO.

Cahill, Jack (1985) 'Culture shock', *Toronto Star*, 23 November 1985: B1–B6.

Eagleton, Terry (1990) 'Nationalism: irony and commitment', in Eagleton, Jameson and Said, (1990): 23–39.

Eagleton, Terry, Jameson, Fredric and Said, Edward (1990) *Nationalism, Colonialism and Literature*. Minneapolis: University of Minnesota Press.

Femmamatics (L. Hissey, A. Hern, L. McLarty) (1989) 'Alice does or situational reflexivity: toward a theory of active female spectators'. Paper presented at Canadian Communication Association, Victoria, 1990.

Flohill, Richard (1988) 'A televised debate: how GATT and free trade may change the way the business of music works in Canada', *The Canadian Composer*, April 1988: 18–22.

Innis, Harold [1950] (1972) *Empire and Communications*. Toronto: University of Toronto Press.

Jephcott, Samuel C. (1985) 'Free trade in the eyes of the U.S.', *The Globe and Mail*, 14 December 1985.

Leblanc, Larry (1990) 'The Canadian record industry 1990'. Report to the Department of Communications, Ottawa, Canada.

Murphy, Brian (1983) *The World Wired Up: Unscrambling the new communications puzzle*. London: Comedia.

Nelson, Joyce (1986) 'Losing it in the lobby: on free trade, entertainment and Quebec's Bill 109', *This Magazine*, October/November 1986: 14–23.

Patrick, Lannie (1989) 'Global economy, global communication: the Canada-U.S. free trade agreement', in Raboy and Bruck (1989).

Raboy, Marc and Bruck, Peter (1989) editors, *Communication: For and Against Democracy*. Montreal: Black Rose Books.

Smith, Anthony (1980) *The Geopolitics of Information: How Western Culture Dominates the World*. New York: Oxford University Press.

Jody Berland is Assistant Professor of Communications Studies at Concordia University in Montreal

REEBEE GAROFALO

THE INTERNATIONALIZATION OF THE US MUSIC INDUSTRY AND ITS IMPACT ON CANADA

Ever since the Edison phonograph was first demonstrated to enthusiastic audiences in Europe and Canada in 1878, a few months after its invention, the US recording industry has benefited from the exploitation of its international connections. The first Canadian-made commercial recordings featuring Canadian talent, for example, were made in 1900 by the Canadian subsidiary of the Emile Berliner Company, the forerunner of RCA Victor. Still, the systematic exploitation of the world market *as a condition of further growth* is a phenomenon which did not become dominant until the 1980s. Let me begin by setting the stage for this development.

By the early eighties, disco, then the defining sound of US pop, had begun to collapse under its own weight, aided significantly by hard-rock racism and a more legitimate aesthetic aversion to the relentless thumping of the 120 beats-per-minute formula. Punk, which earlier had infused the industry with a potential energy not seen in popular music since the 1960s, was born again as new wave. By the early eighties, it had incorporated such diverse musical elements, including disco itself, that it became virtually unrecognizable as a genre. At this point, the marketing categories of the US industry were temporarily thrown into disarray. For a time, the term 'new music' was used to describe everybody from Blondie to Michael Jackson.

During this period, the US music industry also suffered its first recession in thirty years. Revenues from the sale of recorded music in the USA declined from an all-time high of $4.1 billion in 1978 to a low of $3.6 billion in 1982 (RIAA, 1986: 4). This was a fairly dramatic decrease for an industry that had more than doubled in size from 1973 to 1978. The industry responded by laying off hundreds of workers and by cutting back significantly on production. Whereas there had been 4,170 new LPs released in 1978, by 1984 that number had declined to 2,170 (RIAA, 1986: 5). With the number of new releases in the US cut literally in half, production became significantly more restrictive, making it harder for new artists to break into the market.

It was in this context that technological advances – most notably the full deployment of satellite transmission – created the possibility of instant national exposure for recording artists as well as the simultaneous broadcast of performances on a worldwide scale. In the US, this capability first manifested itself in the creation of the most powerful music outlet ever to be developed – MTV, launched on 1 August 1981 by Warner-Amex. MTV quickly became the fastest growing cable channel in history and was unquestionably the most effective way for a record to get national exposure. With 85 per cent of its viewers between twelve and thirty-four years old, MTV also delivered the perfect consumers for a tight economy. And if record-company production was restrictive, MTV's programming policies were downright exclusionary. 'On MTV's current roster of some 800 acts,' reported one survey in 1983, '16 are black' (*People*, 1983: 3).

Initially, MTV even refused to air the video of Michael Jackson's 'Billie Jean'. Whether it was the overwhelming popularity of the record which changed MTV's mind or the widespread, but officially denied, rumor that CBS threatened to pull all of its music videos from MTV unless they aired the Jackson tape, the fact is that 'Billie Jean', followed by 'Beat It' and 'Thriller', soon became some of the most popular videos ever aired on MTV.

It was in fact the unprecedented success of the 'Thriller' LP which contributed significantly to the economic recovery of the industry as a whole. It wasn't until 1984, with sales of $4.4 billion, that the US music industry once again reached its 1978 level. By this time, 'Thriller', released in 1983, had earned a place in the *Guinness Book of Records* as the largest-selling LP of all time, eventually reaching sales of some forty million units worldwide. 'Thriller' underscored two of the most salient aspects of the industry's recovery: concentration of product and expansion into new markets. With respect to the former, economic recovery, according to *Billboard*, 'was due more to the runaway success of a handful of smash hits than to an across-the-board pickup in album sales' (*Billboard*, 1984: 4). 'Thriller' thus signalled an era of blockbuster LPs featuring a limited number of superstar artists as the solution to the industry's economic woes.

While the recession was real enough in financial terms, it may have been attributable, in part, to a simple levelling-off of sales due to a saturation of the domestic market. Having anticipated this dimension of the crisis, US record companies embarked on an aggressive campaign aimed at international sales. As early as 1977, both CBS and RCA were reporting that more than 50 per cent of their sales came from their international divisions but, in these instances, the figures resulted from international artists like Julio Iglesias outselling domestic product. In the 1980s, the strategy for internationalization centered around the systematic exportation of music that was produced *for* the domestic market.

Paradoxically, the record companies were aided significantly in this quest by a most unlikely set of players—artists with a social conscience. By the mid-eighties, the combination of technology making the world a smaller place and superstars reaching out to larger international audiences created a new awareness of world problems. This awareness expressed itself most dramatically in the phenomenon of mega-events – that string of socially conscious mass concerts and all-star performances beginning with Band Aid, USA for Africa, and Live Aid which was dubbed, in true liberal fashion, 'charity rock'. It was charity rock which caused the world to stand up and take notice of the extent to which the power of popular music could be harnessed in the service of social and political causes. It was also through charity rock that Anglo-American Top Forty was broadcast to hundreds of millions of people in every corner of the globe. While most observers agreed, however reluctantly, that mega-events had a generally progressive effect, the concerts were also heavily criticized as yet another example of Anglo-American cultural imperialism.

To be sure, one must be aware of the negative effects of exporting US culture in terms of overwhelming local cultures and supplanting indigenous musics. Indeed, the US military now uses popular music to announce its presence in foreign lands. Still, the cultural imperialism thesis is simply not adequate to explain the social relations of exporting US pop. Unlike, say, film or video, popular music is seldom exported as a finished product. What gets exported most often are master tapes which require the development of a whole production and distribution infrastructure within the host country. This process plays some role in building the local economy. But, more importantly, in order to operate cost effectively, the local production facilities are also utilized for the production of local musics. There is, thus, an interaction between US pop and local musics which isn't found in the exportation of other mass cultural forms. This interaction does not negate the destructive tendencies of cultural domination, but is does hold out the possibility that even Anglo-American influences can be appropriated to advantage by the host country. Far from simply being overwhelmed by outside influences, there have been many instances – for example, reggae, salsa, high life, and mbaqanga – where local musics have incorporated outside elements in ways that have actually strengthened the indigenous culture.

The context in which mega-events took place provided a moment of opportunity, albeit a limited one, wherein internationalization was a two-way process. While Anglo-American music was exposed to the world in what was generally intended to be a unidirectional process, certain foreign artists such as Youssou N'Dour also gained some access to the coveted US market.

Finally, to the extent that cultural imperialism is a prop for economic domination, it must be noted that in the case of the exportation of US pop, the United States is no longer the main beneficiary of the profits. Of the five largest transnational recording companies, only one of them, Time Warner, remains in US hands. Still, it is Anglo-American popular music which dominates the international market. And, in the case of Canada, there is a particular structural dependency on the US industry.

Since the beginnings of recording and broadcasting, Canada has been dominated by foreign-owned companies, mainly those based in the USA. Even before the turn of the century, all three major US recording companies

– Edison, Columbia, and Berliner (later, Victor) – had Canadian subsidiaries which controlled the lion's share of the Canadian market. To this day, not a single Canadian-owned record company operates its own national distribution network even though distribution has been a key to profitability since the 1960s. At best, Canadian labels can avail themselves of independent regional distribution or the Canadian-based (but largely US-owned) East-West national distribution link that dates back to the establishment of the railroads. Now, the Free Trade Agreement (FTA) threatens the only national distribution network on Canadian soil by making it potentially easier and more profitable for US companies to service Canada from the northern United States, as protective tariffs are gradually eliminated over the next decade. Such a development could even cause US firms to question the wisdom of maintaining large subsidiary labels in Canada at all.

The historical situation in broadcasting has been similar. Although commercial broadcasting began in 1920 in both Canada and the United States, the USA was soon broadcasting on almost all of the available channels, including those reserved for Canadian use. US firms also owned and operated most of the 'clear channels' – frequencies positioned to broadcast over great distances with minimal interference. By the time Canada's prestigious Royal Commission on Radio Broadcasting, chaired by Sir John Aird, issued its 1929 final report, which recommended a government-owned system based on the British model, privately owned Canadian stations had already affiliated with the NBC and CBS networks based in the US. The Canadian-content laws of the early seventies reflected the tension between independent Canadian record labels, who were trying to make a go of it promoting Canadian artists, and Canadian radio stations, who found it far more profitable to broadcast US pop.

Structural ties to the USA have had a profound effect on Canadian artist development and, therefore, the character of Canadian music. In the early 1900s, Canadian recording artists were often recorded outside of Canada. This trend continued into the rock era as top-selling Canadian artists from Paul Anka, the Crew Cuts, and the Diamonds in the fifties to Joni Mitchell, and Neil Young in the sixties recorded south of their native borders to achieve fame and fortune. At present, the direct signing of artists like Jeff Healey (Arista), Colin James (Virgin), Pursuit of Happiness (Chrysalis), Dan Hill (Columbia), and k. d. lang (Sire) to US parent companies, rather than to their Canadian subsidiaries, is perceived as making it much harder for Canadian labels to sign talent.

Interestingly, the Canadian music industry had two of its best years ever in 1988 and 1989, with sales totalling $700 million and $750 million respectively. Proponents of the FTA were quick to point out that major labels had invested a record $20 million in Canadian talent in 1989. Some even speculated that if the Canadian dollar remained weak compared to its US counterpart, then with the decline of tariffs, some US labels might look to less inexpensive Canadian firms to do their manufacturing. Cinram Ltd, Canada's largest record manufacturer, even gained a foothood in the US with the purchase of the PRC Tape company, enabling them to sell direct to the US market. On the other hand, the 175-store Atlantique Video and Sound chain went bankrupt, as did The Music Brokers, one of Canada's largest independent music-promotion firms. After all was said and done, it had to be admitted that the entire growth of the Canadian industry was simply a function of increased CD penetration, rather than a general increase in unit sales. And, in September 1990, the CD showed its first-ever decline in Canadian sales. For top-selling Canadian artists such as Kim Mitchell and Rita MacNeil, the upshot of all of this was that the US market looked as attractive, and elusive, as ever.

The US market is and has always been ten times larger than the Canadian market. From a financial point of view, it is almost impossible for a successful Canadian artist not to think about the US market. For this reason, it is often the case that Canadian artists who are perceived as being able to 'make it' are groomed for the US market. But, direct connections abroad do not always work to an artist's benefit. In certain areas, such as the video market, they can actually be harmful. Given the more stringent rules for Canadian content in video, which now require that a video either be produced or directed by a Canadian or videotaped in Canada, foreign-made videos which don't make it as hits cannot then be played in Canada as Canadian content. At present, this is a major consideration since MuchMusic (owned by CHUM Ltd) – Canada's creatively superior counterpart to MTV – is currently the most effective promotional outlet for Canadian artists.

Once perceived as well outside the Canadian music industry establishment, MuchMusic's comparatively unrestricted playlist forced radio to open up its programming to some degree. The channel's recent switch to basic cable is expected to quadruple its audience and, according to a graduated provision in its license agreement, 30 per cent of its videos must now be Canadian content. The presence of MuchMusic has spurred the development of Musique Plus, a French-language equivalent, and contributed to the establishment of a $5 million government fund, 40 per cent of which is earmarked for French-language music, to assist artists with record and video production.

Still, there is a sense in which even the somewhat unorthodox MuchMusic falls prey to ideological influences from the US, no differently than the rest of the Canadian music industry. When MuchMusic held its awards ceremony this year, the award categories included rap, country, soul, MOR, heavy metal, and dance music, among others. Canadian artists compete even for domestic recognition in categories that are defined within and by the US music industry. To the extent that marketing categories shape the nature of artist development and musical style, Canadian music necessarily evolves along lines that are determined by US music. This process not only devalues Canadian traditions at home, it also places Canadian artists in the position of competing for wider recognition on US terms. In the end, one has to wonder whether, in fact, there is a sound that can be considered distinctly Canadian.

If this situation is difficult for Canadian artists in general, it is doubly hard for Francophone artists who are faced with the pressure of recording in English in order to achieve broader appeal. When Celine Dion, at twenty-one a veteran of the Quebec music scene, made her recent bid for international stardom, she did so on the strength of her first all-English LP, 'Unison'. While it is noteworthy, if somewhat opportunistic, that she publicly refused to accept this year's Felix award for Anglophone Artist of the Year, it is clear that, to some extent, her career choices were subject to the dictates of US tastemakers.

If Canada seeks to offer the world a music that is distinctly Canadian, it can only do so in terms that are defined by Canadians. Alternatively, Canada must recognize and deal with the reality that it is a lesser partner in what is essentially a North American music industry dominated by the USA. This latter vision entails focusing the struggle on such inequalities of the system as the fact that English-speaking Canadian artists are dreadfully underfinanced as compared to their US counterparts and that non-English-speaking musics are relegated to the margins of the industry. Such struggles are, in many ways, analogous to the battles fought by African-American and Latin-American artists within the USA.

References

Billboard (1984) 14 January.
People Magazine (1983) 4 April.
RIAA (Recording Industry Association of America) (1986) *Inside The Recording Industry: A Statistical Overview*. New York.

Reebee Garofalo teaches at the University of Boston and is the co-author of Rock 'n' Roll is Here to Pay

SARA COHEN

POPULAR MUSIC AND URBAN REGENERATION: THE MUSIC INDUSTRIES OF MERSEYSIDE

This paper discusses popular music and urban regeneration initiatives in Liverpool, a city based within the Merseyside region. The paper is divided into three sections. The first gives some background to these initiatives; the second outlines a few of them, concentrating largely upon those instigated and supported by Liverpool City Council. Such initiatives raise many issues and problems. The paper does not attempt to suggest solutions, but the third section outlines several research projects currently being undertaken at Liverpool University's Institute of Popular Music. These projects address some of these problems through an emphasis on locality and the need to appreciate the historical and social situation of musicians and other cultural producers and consumers when developing initiatives in response to changes or trends at a national or international level.

Background

The debate over the contribution of the arts to the regeneration of the inner cities entered the national agenda in Britain in the second half of the 1980s. Research suggests that, rather than being seen as a subsidized adjunct to the economy, the arts and cultural industries should be recognized as having an increasingly important role within it. It was in cities controlled by left-wing Labour councils – such as Sheffield, Birmingham and Glasgow – that arts and cultural industries initiatives first became a visible part of local responses to the decline of manufacturing industries and steep rises in unemployment. The Arts Council and the Conservative Government have also emphasized the substantial contribution that the arts can make to the revitalization of urban areas, although the Government – in keeping with its economic policy – has severely cut its subsidy to the arts and has been trying to encourage local authorities to look to the private sector for such support.

British cities and towns are now increasingly including the arts in their programmes of economic, physical and social regeneration, largely because the arts is one of the few areas that can still be supported (indirectly) from a mixture of European, Central and Local government funds – funds often limited to certain types of urban development initiatives, such as those involving buildings or training. Many local authorities are therefore concentrating upon renovating city centres, and upon training and tourism. These strategies are generally consumer- rather than production-based, and while some have been led by the public sector, others depend upon partnerships between the public and private sectors. Some initiatives continue to focus upon the more traditional or 'high' arts, while others have defined the arts more broadly to emphasize community involvement or to include the cultural industries. Only recently, however, has popular music been included. Unlike classical music, it has developed as a commercial form treated with disdain by public policy. Now, however, some local authorities have begun to recognize its economic and social potential. So far, their popular-music initiatives are based around the trends identified above and follow a similar pattern.

LIVERPOOL

For the past three decades Liverpool has been renowned throughout the world for its popular music and successful artists, yet it has an extremely dilapidated music industry from which hardly anyone in the city is making any profit. Liverpool's tragedy, as perceived by many, is that its bands have traditionally left the city as soon as they have become successful and have consequently invested nothing in it. An often-quoted statistic is the £200 million supposedly grossed by Frankie Goes to Hollywood during the first year of their success, virtually none of which benefited Liverpool. The Beatles have been continually criticized for their lack of investment in the city, and Liverpool has, in addition, failed to capitalize upon them as a tourist attraction.

However, it is not just musicians that have left. Since the early 1960s, Liverpool has lost a third of its population and nearly half of its jobs. Unemployment rates are 70–80 per cent in some areas and the city has little employment-generating industry of its own. It has a high, but not very flattering media profile (national newspapers and TV channels exhibit almost an obsession and certainly a fascination with it, attributing to it a sense of exoticism and repeatedly using it in plays and documentaries as a colourful backdrop to inner-city decline). This national media image has built upon a general sense of oppression and of being 'hard-done-by' within the city, and has emphasized a sense of local identity, loyalty, and defiance to the outside world. This is fuelled by the local media, which criticize local celebrities if they discredit the city in any way.

Nevertheless, there remains a tradition of leaving among local rock musicians, one which results from a combination of ideology and necessity, and which – through increased interest in urban regeneration and the cultural industries – has recently become more of an issue. Other British cities have also lost artists to London, but, in recent times, musicians from such cities as Manchester, Sheffield, Glasgow and Dublin have publicly broadcast their commitment to, and investment in, those cities. (A couple of years ago various councillors and arts officials from Liverpool visited Sheffield's new audio-visual enterprise centre and, more recently, Manchester's leading popular-music entrepreneur visited Liverpool University to address an audience of local musicians. On both occasions the commitment of local musicians to those respective cities was almost flaunted, and the absence of commitment from Liverpool's native musicians highlighted.)

Liverpool's problem, therefore, is often perceived as being not so much one of how to promote talent and activity in the city, but, rather, that of how to encourage successful local bands to *stay* in the city, how to improve the city's music industry so that it can capitalize upon their earnings, and how to use popular music in other ways to regenerate the local economy. Over the last three years, approaches to this problem have come from local government, education and the private sector. Most of the major initiatives so far have been public-sector led. In Great Britain, city councils control public spending at local-government level. The relationship of such councils (particularly Labour-controlled councils) to central government can be problematic, and, in this regard, the situation of Liverpool is notorious. Liverpool City Council has consistently been at the forefront of opposition to certain aspects of government policy, and one particular confrontation in 1987, led to the demise of the Militant-led council and the rise to power of a new Labour group.

While the previous council had not prioritized arts, cultural policy, or economic development itself, the new council emphasized the need for a complete rethinking of the city's economic and social infrastructure, conceiving a future rooted in a service-based economy wherein tourism, high technology, arts and the cultural industries would play a major role. Liverpool's Arts and Cultural Industries Strategy was published in 1987, considerably later than those of other major cities in Britain. It adopted a broad definition of the arts and cultural industries, one which encompassed 'those social practices whose primary purpose is the transmission of meaning'. Its key objective was 'to maximize the contribution which the arts and cultural industries make to the economic *and* social well-being of the city', thus placing the emphasis upon business and employment development, and upon community involvement, the provision of services, and more general quality-of-life issues.

In Liverpool the problems of implementing such a strategy are particularly acute. The city is rife with tensions, one example of which is the split within Liverpool between areas controlled by the city council, and the waterfront areas managed by Merseyside Development Corporation, which is financed through a combination of central-government and private funds. These conflicts between public and private sectors, and local and central governments, are sharpened by particular socio-economic conditions in the city. Also, the private sector is small and business sponsorship for the arts is thus limited. Moreover, the dismantling of regional support for the arts (in the form of Merseyside County Council and the Regional Arts Association) has led to fragmentation. Local arts organizations are now accountable to a confusing array of authorities such that the integration of arts and leisure provision is difficult. There is also some wariness of council involvement in the arts on the part of those working in arts-related areas, because of the council's support – in the past – for some unsuccessful schemes, and its inefficiency in carrying out such basic services as rubbish collection. At the time of writing, the city council is facing the worst financial position any local authority has had to face for years, with the prospect of huge job cuts and a disruption of services. Liverpool is effectively bankrupt. It faces a shortfall of at least £12.1 million, and it is fighting an uphill battle to attract investment.

Liverpool's identity and heritage are, nevertheless, already strongly linked to culture and the city has several major assets: museums and art galleries, impressive Georgian and Victorian architecture, and a strong reputation in the performing arts – in particular, music, comedy and the theatre. The city council has recently taken some innovative steps to capitalize upon these assets, appointing Britain's first municipal Film Liaison Officer, for example, and investing directly in the production of a film (the first time a local authority has ever done this). The council's music-related initiatives have also been bold and the following section of the paper outlines a few of these.

Popular music initiatives

CITY BEAT

In 1987, the council commissioned a report to define a role for the music industry in its Arts and Cultural Industries Strategy. The resulting document proposed that the council establish a management and promotions company to identify, develop and market local talent, deal with legal and publishing matters on behalf of the artists involved, and encourage the development of a private-sector music industry in Liverpool. The company – called City Beat – would consist of six staff and would be managed by a board of city councillors and representatives from other funding agencies. It would be a nonprofit, limited liability company, as the profit made would be reinvested in the project and other, similar cultural industries initiatives.

The proposal attracted criticism, particularly from those already engaged in similar music-management and development enterprises who had not been consulted by the council. It was felt that the proposed agency would be in direct competition with other local businesses; that too much money would be concentrated on too few people; that the structure was too bureaucratic in a business where spontaneity and quick decision-making were paramount; that there weren't enough people with the necessary experience left in Liverpool to run such a company; and that the agency's existence would be threatened when a new council was elected. The estimate of a 30 per cent success rate for the artists involved was also thought to be naive, given that, on average, fewer than 1 per cent of local bands ever receive a record contract, and fewer of those achieve subsequent success.

MUSIC CITY

One of the main critics was the manager of two well-known local bands. In response, the council commissioned this person to produce, over a twelve-month period, another report which would examine existing resources and services in the region's music industries, address the long-term development of these industries, and explore the potential for investment-seeking partnerships between the city council and other agencies. This Manager appointed a core group of three consultants – himself, a Branch manager of the National Westminster Bank, and myself (a Research Fellow at Liverpool University's Institute of Popular Music), along with a part-time administrator. The report, entitled 'Music City', adopts a broad definition of the music industries, and deals with a variety of musical styles, including classical. Its submission is now, for various reasons (including the development of other initiatives to be discussed shortly), one year overdue. The final report will comprise a series of separately commissioned studies. In brief, these are likely to include:

1. a comprehensive survey of the region's music industries;
2. a survey and analysis of music-industry training needs and provision;
3. the case for establishing a music-industry information centre and database in the city;
4. an investigation into the benefits of music-led cultural exchanges and international twinning, focusing in particular upon New Orleans and Leningrad;
5. a feasibility study on an annual international music festival (which the city council had identified as a possible key component in both its tourism and arts and cultural industries strategies);
6. a reappraisal of the original idea of a city-council-sponsored agency for local music development, and an examination of alternative models, such as the establishment of a Music Industry Development and Advisory Service.

OTHER INITIATIVES

After the Music City Report had been commissioned, several music-related initiatives developed and it became part of the Music City brief to co-ordinate, advise upon, or monitor them. There were roughly five notable initiatives, the three most important are outlined below.

The John Lennon concert

The John Lennon concert was staged in May 1990, to mark what would have been the 50th birthday of John Lennon and the 10th anniversary of his death. Liverpool was selected as the venue from a short-list of five cities which included New York, Los Angeles and Tokyo. The concert was seen by the city council as a major profile-raising event for Liverpool, which would lay the foundation for future events and place Liverpool 'on the map' in terms of live-music presentation. The council was keen to involve local cultural industries in it.

Charterhouse

The role that some kind of cultural quarter or district could play in the council's Arts and Cultural Industries Strategy had been considered. Other cities have developed such quarters in order to revitalize their cultural night-life and evening economy, and to foster a community of inter-related businesses which would complement, co-operate with and benefit from each other. Some arts officials felt, however, that such a quarter wouldn't suit Liverpool, largely because there were already cultural enterprises within the city which were fragmented and under-resourced, but which, nevertheless, embodied a tradition of individualism that might lead them to resent what they might see as a form of 'co-ordination' or stage-management (or even exclusivity).

However, the council has been forced into selling areas of land in order to finance its operations, and it recently sold off a large sector of the city centre, incorporating many listed buildings, to Charterhouse – a London development company – for just £7 million. The company proposes to make this sector a cultural quarter, with a focus upon music.

Liverpool Institute of Performing Arts

What is particularly interesting in Liverpool, at the moment, is the role which certain educational institutions are attempting to play in the arts and cultural industries areas. This is a very recent development, one rooted in the growing pressure on those involved in education to provide more vocational and flexible programmes. An awareness, on the part of educators, central and local governments, of the potential offered by training in popular music has been evident only in the past few years. Most training has thus far been provided largely on an informal and short-term basis.

The Liverpool Institute of Performing Arts initiative followed the establishment of the School of Performing Arts in London, one of several new City Technology Colleges set up with government and private-sector funds. (The School of Performing Arts, for example, was supported by the British Phonographic Industry). The idea for an institute in Liverpool was spearheaded by Paul McCartney, whose main concern was that it should be housed in his old school (which is now empty). A feasibility study on the Institute was co-ordinated by the School of Performing Arts Trust in London, with financial assistance from Paul McCartney, Liverpool City Council and central government's Training Agency. Researchers from London, and one from Liverpool, investigated the training requirements of the relevant industries, surveyed existing and proposed performing arts provision in Liverpool, and considered means of ensuring the institute's credibility as a 'centre of excellence', while at the same time offering as 'open' community access as possible. They subsequently proposed a model unlike that of the City Technology College, one which would attract private sponsors but also suit the city council's political and educational priorities. The model focused on popular music, and included a 'World Music Centre' aimed at visiting international musicians.

TENSIONS

The three major initiatives described all involved the city council working in some capacity with agencies from outside the city. Together, these initiatives exemplify attempts to use popular music to accomplish a wide range of objectives: attracting tourists, providing training, generating employment, improving the image of a city, benefiting the local community, and building bridges to local, national and international contexts. At the same time, however, all of these initiatives have highlighted and emphasized the particular conflicts or tensions that often surface over arts-led regeneration initiatives. These include the following:

1 Firstly, they heightened a wariness, on the part of local people, towards developments imposed from without. In a place like Liverpool, sensitivity to such interference is particularly high, yet restrictions on financing by central government have inevitably intensified the power struggle over resources between central government, local authorities, local residents and outside private developers. When the sale to Charterhouse was publicized, many were dismayed that such a valuable part of the city's heritage had been sold to a London company, a company which, furthermore, had never previously been involved with a development of such scale.

2 Secondly, the initiatives again raised scepticism over the city council's ability to operate effectively with regard to the music industries. Like many local authorities, it is organizationally ill-equipped and inadequately structured to work in this area and is hampered by a lack of co-ordination between its departments. This was brought home by the John Lennon concert. Representatives of the local music industry alleged that the city council lacked the appropriate legal and negotiating skills to deal with the music-business lawyers and promoters involved, with the result that the city lost out on revenue benefits. The concert was promoted by a company based in London that had little knowledge of the city. Only one local band appeared, and local industries were hardly used at all. The plan to have other local events surrounding the concert and capitalizing upon it failed, although a rival, protest event involving local bands did go ahead on the same night. Ticket prices were also high, which deterred local residents, and the charitable Foundation which was linked with the concert and was supposed to distribute revenues from it to the local

community proved to be rather elusive. The costs of the event to the city have now risen to £400,000.

3. The John Lennon concert thus highlighted antagonism towards initiatives which seem to be aimed largely at tourists rather than local residents. It was successful as a television event, and it did attract visitors from abroad, but it was seen to have little relation to the local community.

4. Fourthly, such initiatives often intensify an antagonism towards high-prestige developments in the city centre which threaten grass-roots activity on the periphery. Many working in the local music industries, for example, felt that although the Performing Arts Institute might promote the city's image abroad, it might also contribute very little to the locality. A glamorous development such as this could concentrate resources and attention to the detriment of local studios and arts organizations and activity spread across the region. Linked to this is the attraction of local authorities – particularly in Liverpool – to bold initiatives which will give the city a high profile. Unless handled carefully, however, such initiatives tend to be controversial, arousing hostility within the city and a resentment of intervention by local authorities (as demonstrated by the City Beat proposal).

5. Above all, those working in the music industry feel that agencies in the public, private and education sectors either lack an appreciation of popular music – which still tends to be regarded as frivolous and dangerous – or do not understand the peculiar nature of the industry, problems deemed to be evident in the City Beat and Performing Arts Institute initiatives. The latter proposes to provide training for jobs that don't exist. Recording-studio owners, in particular, point to the vast number of requests for placements they receive from local youths relative to the low number of studio-based jobs. The Institute is envisaged as a future 'launching pad' to London which will have no direct input into local jobs and businesses. Many feel that money going into it would be far better spent on improving the infrastructure of the local music industry, which would *then* generate growth and employment.

(It should be pointed out here that, as far as one can tell, the British Phonographic Industry's motives for getting involved in the London school were mixed, though a commitment to education is unlikely to have been a major factor. The music industry remains generally sceptical about the role of training – most employees receive on-the-job training – and it will be interesting to see how the relationship between it and education establishments will develop.)

6. Finally, these and other initiatives also tend to highlight tensions between business and quality-of-life issues, and the problem of choosing between an emphasis upon consumption or production. The Music City report will propose a major arts festival that can strike a balance between all these issues (*and* involve both tourists and local residents), although it is feared that the John Lennon concert may have jeopardized this proposal. In general, however, the initiatives in Liverpool are consumption-led, and this inevitably leaves certain developments vulnerable to factors beyond

local control, such as shifts in air fares, currency exchange rates and the disposable income of residents.

These tensions and dichotomies demonstrate a fundamental problem. Obviously, those operating within each of the three areas identified – local government, education and the private sector – have their own strategies for coping with, and responding to, changes at the local, national and international levels. They have, as well, their own agendas *vis-à-vis* the arts and cultural industries, and distinctive ways of viewing each other. Inevitably, this leads to differences of ambition and priorities, and to power struggles. Those with access to resources and channels of influence normally impose their initiatives upon the other players without prior negotiation. Each sector also embraces a set of particular discourses whose confrontation often results in misunderstandings or hostility.

This may be directly observed at meetings between the different interest groups involved, such as that organized by the Institute of Popular Music between those responsible for setting up the Performing Arts Institute and representatives from the local music industries, or those between city councillors and music-industry employees subsequent to the City Beat proposal having been publicized. Far from bridging the gap between these groups, these meetings served to underscore them. I have experienced similar situations at Music City meetings, where the discourses of a bank manager, a university research fellow and the manager of rock bands embody a whole range of conflicting perspectives and values with the result that agreement, compromise and clarity become difficult.

The concrete historical and social effects of such conflicting perspectives are evident in the case study (which can only be outlined here in brief) of a frustrating and drawn-out set of circumstances involving one particular studio-based production company in Liverpool. After several years of struggling to survive within the city, this company managed to raise investment from the venture capital branch of a Manchester bank. (This investment was to be matched by small grants from central and local government and by a loan from the company's own bank). The case study shows, however, that, for the past eighteen months, this funding has been jeopardized by the city council and other public and private agencies in Liverpool.

Over the past twenty years, the experiences of the company's staff have left them with a particular perspective on music training and production – a perspective embodying something of a local co-operative and collective ethos *within* Thatcher's enterprise culture – and on their future role in the music industry at the local, national and international levels. This experience has endowed them, as well, with a strong sense of loyalty and commitment to the city. At the same time, however, this company has confronted a local authority that has been able to offer them little in the way of support over the past two years, despite its Arts and Cultural Industries Strategy. That strategy is still in its early stages, but the study reveals that, in trying to encourage growth within the music industries, the city council, along with other agencies in the public and private sector, has, unintentionally, been impeding it.

The constraints placed upon local authorities, and those suffered by Liverpool City Council in particular, obviously limit and restrict the range of initiatives that may be developed within the arts and cultural industries. The initiatives described above are problematic and intersect with wider national and transnational issues that are not locally determined. These cases do illustrate, however, the importance of an understanding of, and sensitivity to, locality. The following section will take up this theme, with reference to work being undertaken at the Institute of Popular Music.

The Institute of Popular Music and local research projects

The Institute of Popular Music was set up by the University of Liverpool in 1988 to provide a specialist centre for the study of popular music. It employs two staff: David Horn, the Director, and myself. As a new agency in the city, we, too, are required to address the relationship between popular music and urban regeneration, and to define our particular role in this area. Unlike the Liverpool Institute of Performing Arts, we did not immediately launch ourselves in a high-profile manner and impose an agenda when we entered the local arena. We have tried, instead, to respond more cautiously to local needs and, as a new agency (and yet another outsider), have been able to act as a catalyst for various local initiatives and to help organize and co-ordinate particular events and activities.

We have also collaborated with the Music City report, although until the city council responds to it, it will be difficult to know what the council thinks about the future role of popular music in the city and what we should do to try and help. In the meantime, we are progressing with teaching, information, the development of archive and library resources, and research. It is too early to tell whether our current progress in these areas will help at all, but I would like to outline, very briefly, a few of the local research projects underway, and indicate ways in which, supplemented by case studies, they might contribute and perhaps complement future proposals and initiatives.

THE MUSIC CITY SURVEY

Together with a research assistant, I carried out a survey on the current state of the music industries on Merseyside for the Music City report. This involved:

1. looking at the geographical and numerical distribution of these industries;
2. compiling a directory of resources and services;
3. assessing the current economic impact of the industries on the local economy as measured by the purchase of local goods and services, local

employment, the annual rate of turnover, and level of local investment of profits;
4 identifying the industries' current and future skills-training needs;
5 surveying the attitudes of industry managers and practitioners towards their own company growth prospects, their preferred areas for public and private investment, and the current assistance (financial and other) that they receive.

The final report also included the following: a summary of local activity and provision of services according to different musical styles; general conclusions concerning trends, developments and gaps in provision; and a list of recommendations and suggestions for future research and initiatives.

THE 'LOCAL SOUNDS' RESEARCH PROJECT

Recently, we began a three-month research project which aims to investigate the concept of a local sound. Today, much is written about the way in which rock music has been at the forefront of a process of cultural homogenization, breaking through international barriers and leading to what some call a 'global village' effect. Postmodernists talk of an age of cultural mixing, blending, borrowing, and stealing – all aided by recent developments in technology. Nevertheless, people in Britain still continue to talk in terms of local sounds, linking particular musical styles with particular localities and with the various characteristics and stereotypes associated with those areas. In Liverpool, for example, the preoccupation with a 'Liverpool sound' has continued since the 1960s, not just in the music press, but among musicians and non-musicians from Liverpool and elsewhere.

Definitions and descriptions of this sound are wide-ranging and contradictory, giving rise to much debate and scepticism as to its distinctiveness or even existence. However, cultural forms originate within, interact with, and are inevitably affected by, the physical, social, political and economic factors which surround them. So it is this broader and more complex issue of the relationship between music and place that will be investigated, not just the construction, promotion and manipulation of particular local sounds. The project will involve groups of local musicians and journalists listening to and discussing music. These meetings will be supplemented by additional research involving, for example, lyrical and musicological analysis, surveys of local consumers and producers, and an examination of record sales.

LOCAL HISTORY PROJECT

Another research project with which the Institute of Popular Music is currently involved is a six-month pilot study on popular music in twentieth-century Liverpool, conducted with financial support from Liverpool University and the National Museums and Galleries on Merseyside (which hitherto have paid little attention to the cultural life of the city). The study aims to: (a) map the major historical and social changes involving popular music that have occurred in Liverpool in this century; (b) undertake an inventory of existing resources; and (c) test the various types of evidence and appropriate ways of collecting and archiving it. The project involves a case study on kinship (incorporating an oral history) which examines the musical experiences of families from different social groups in the city in order to highlight changes in the production and consumption of music, and to analyze the complex and dynamic relationship between music, memory and the past. An exhibition based on the study will open in July 1991 and will involve a publication, a video and a larger series of talks and performances. The archive resulting from the project will serve as both documentation centre and community resource.

Conclusion

The point has been made (e.g., by Wallis and Malm, 1984) that contemporary popular music is characterized by increased globalization on the one hand and increased localization on the other, as developments in communications and technology allow local populations greater access to music production and consumption. There are, of course, other readings of this polarity, such as the argument that locality only matters now *because of* the globalization process, and that emphasizing place in the midst of the increasing abstraction of space reveals a kind of quest for security in a shifting, uncertain age (Harvey, 1989). The research projects outlined above indicate the importance of locality in other senses and may be significant in several respects:

1 The *survey of local music industries* was conducted part time over a three-month period. There isn't sufficient space here to discuss the methods used, but research such as this inevitably involves a lot of problems, and we have not yet encountered a similar survey conducted anywhere in Britain. The music industry is characterized by a wide variety and diversity of skills and businesses (ranging, for example, from free-lance, part-time individuals to large retail chains). Many businesses are also involved with non-musical activities and found it difficult to produce figures relating specifically to music. The industry is also very informal – much of the work being part-time, sporadic, cash-in-hand, or unpaid – and very volatile, involving a rapid turnover of businesses, organizations and musical groups. It is competitive and factionalized, which is a strength inasmuch as it is accompanied by a sense of individualism, motivation and ambition, but a weakness in that it often results in a lack of co-ordination and co-operation. These problems were compounded by a sense of cynicism at the idea of city-council involvement, and by the number of other feasibility studies and audits on the arts on Merseyside being carried out at the same time by both local and outside organizations. Despite these problems – and despite the concern of many researchers over the use to which the information gathered will eventually be put, the way that it will be interpreted, and the fact that it is rapidly going out of date – the survey *was* worthwhile, if only for the compilation of the Directory and the process of public consultation (which should be the basis for any local authority's strategy for

regeneration). A survey may also raise levels of consciousness and debate over certain issues, and, in the absence of accurate statistics, the opinions gathered could be used in support of particular initiatives. Also, the greater the extent of people's involvement, the greater the loyalty they may feel to the services eventually provided.

The Directory is in great demand, although it has not yet been properly printed and copied. The information it contains changes so quickly that it needs constant updating, but that information exists in no other form at the moment and we were amazed when conducting the survey at the existing lack of knowledge of services and supplies, even within particular sectors of the industry. In this respect, the Directory alone may do much to promote linkages within the industry. Making use of the music industry without knowing of what it consists is obviously difficult.

2 As a result of this survey, we became increasingly aware of the potential of *case studies* in providing valuable insight into an industry that is notoriously difficult to define and assess, illuminating the complexity of life at this grass-roots level and highlighting the various important issues and processes involved. The studio-based production company mentioned earlier, for example, employs six staff who are paid through an intricately balanced and timed rotation of four or five different government schemes – each of which lasts six to twelve months – through supplementary benefit, and through support from family and friends. The rent, rates and operating costs of the studio are funded through a diverse range of income-generating musical activities and a network of exchange relations whereby, for example, the services of photographers and accountants are paid for in studio time, and a free-lance programmer and arranger has a rent-free room in the building in exchange for the loan of his equipment. Profits generated by the studio are used to fund the production side of the organization.

3 The *pilot study on popular music and local history*, on the other hand, offers a historical dimension that is lacking in Liverpool City Council's Arts and Cultural Industries Strategy. This is not just a matter of archives, heritage and tourism. By highlighting submerged histories and identities the project builds upon a sense of local identity, tradition and civic esteem among local inhabitants and encourages access, by certain marginalized groups, to a local industry that is overwhelmingly white and male. The focus upon kinship offers a new perspective on popular music. One aim of the project is to stimulate reflection on, and an understanding of, the significance of music in people's lives and history, not only through oral history and exhibitions, but through the media, publications and widespread participation in the collection of data.

All of this should complement those initiatives aimed at tourism and other forms of economic regeneration. Their long-term success depends upon the fostering of civic identity, community involvement and the democratization of access to the arts. Tourism, it is said, begins at home. The Beatles and the 'Liverpool sound' they embodied may be important to Liverpool, but they exemplify one among many different sounds within a whole range of musical activities and achievements cutting across many different social groups in Liverpool throughout this century.

In Britain, at the moment, there is the phenomena of the so-called 'Manchester sound', which is depicted as revolving around a particular group of bands and clubs, a distinctive style of fashion and dance, and a specific drug. This has emerged as a new and vibrant scene and been promoted through clever marketing and hype by the local industry and the national press. The whole package is now being exported abroad, with all the associated merchandise. The extent to which this has boosted the image of the city and contributed to Manchester's economy and tourist trade has been debated by academics and journalists. Music, fashion and clubs are now, however, among the city's growth industries; what is, perhaps, surprising is that – unlike museums and the 'high' arts – they are not being exploited or even recognized by the local Tourist Board or local government.

The Manchester phenomenon serves, nevertheless, to illustrate the importance of locality within marketing strategies. The 1980s in Britain became the decade of urban entrepreneurialism and aggressive place-marketing. (Manchester was also packaged in a different form as part of its Olympics bid.) This process of selling particular cities leads to competition between them at a time when regional collaboration would be more beneficial. It also results, perhaps, in the creation and presentation of particular images, sounds, and heritages which marginalize or exclude others.

4 The research projects and case studies outlined here point to the importance of an awareness of – and sensitivity to – locality (and the histories and relationships embodied within it) on the part of public agencies responding to trends at a national or international level. The studies highlight and seek to understand the competing and intersecting identities and discourses that exist among different interest groups at a local level, and this may promote better understanding and communication between these groups (something essential for the success of urban-regeneration initiatives such as those described above). It may even help those groups determine their priorities and targets. What, for example, do they mean by 'the local community'?

5 The studies also emphasize the importance of local identity. The concept of a 'local sound', for example, does not refer simply to the accessibility and activity of music production and consumption at a grass-roots level. It encompasses, as well, the sense of local identity and the concepts of locality or place that people bring to the listening to music which affect the way in which they hear and experience it. My own experiences in Liverpool – particularly in light of current research on family and kinship – indicate that, in this age of global mobility, opportunity, expanding markets, and European integration, cultural producers are still defining themselves and their social space in terms of their particular localities.

6 Finally, micro-studies which focus upon the dynamics of culture and power in local contexts offer a means for examining and illuminating the

aforementioned transnational or macro-level trends. Liverpool is obviously unique at many levels. It has its own peculiar economic, social and political situation and particular sets of attitudes, traditions and histories, and these incorporate distinct sets of relationships between city council and other public and private agencies in the city, and between the city council and the state. But all localities are unique, and they are important because it is through them that broader trends are received and experienced, assimilated or resisted, and reproduced.

References

Harvey, David (1989) *The Condition of Postmodernity*. Oxford: Basil Blackwell.
Wallis, Roger and Krister Malm (1984) *Big Sounds from Small Peoples*. London: Constable & Company.

Sara Cohen is a Research Fellow at the Institute of Popular Music, University of Liverpool, England

LAURIE BROWN

SONGS FROM THE BUSH GARDEN[1]

Someplace or other, the late, great Canadian literary critic Northrop Frye said two things that have made a lot of sense to me as I have thought and talked about 'Canadian culture'. The first is that regionalism is the predominant strength of Canadian artists; and the second, that the Big Question facing Canadian artists is not 'Who am I?' – the one that stumps the Yanks and the Brits – but, rather, 'Where is here?' I know that Frye would sit late at night in his north Toronto house picking out Haydn on his piano, but I have no idea what his views of Canadian popular music might have been. I'd bet the farm, however, that Frye's views of Canadian Literature apply equally well to Canadian Pop and to most other aspects of Canadian Culture.[2]

I want to discuss both regionalism and identity as they relate to Canadian pop music and rock music, and add into the mix – if it's not too audacious to tack on a little something of my own to Norrie's list – the idea of the 'removed' voice. By this I mean that the fact we're still sitting here at the southern fringe of a great frontier, having managed to slip the British yoke and not yet replaced it entirely with the US one, is what gives Canadians a perspective and a voice, to the extent that these exist. And, from out here in Frye's 'bush garden', that removed voice is growing increasingly persuasive, and more and more being heard.

In an essay in his collection *Divisions on a Ground*, Frye argues that Canadian literature – over the course of the 1800s – moved from being a kind of expression of a provincial outpost of imperial Britain to a real and legitimate voice of its own. That is, people writing in Canada originally tended to write about the fact that they were not someplace else – usually not in their bucolic childhood homes in pastoral England. In both content and style, they were essentially colonial – they defined themselves by where they were not.

I'm arguing that much the same kind of development has happened in Canadian popular music. That is, for a great deal of its recorded development, which has only been of any significance since World War II, Canadian popular music was either a pale imitation of the British music hall or a reflection of the brilliance of the Brill Building in New York City. In the past twenty years, however, Canadian popular musicians have found a voice. As it turns out, perhaps not surprisingly, that voice has tended to be folk-inspired and often rural, manifesting itself of late in country music and – even more recently – in country music performed by women.

Can it be shown that this rural, folk-based, often female music is essentially Canadian in its regionalism, a regionalism distinct from that of the US? Simply by definition, regions are self-defined and autonomous and, therefore, a Canadian region is likely to be different from an American region. But, given that regions are often settled along geographic, and not political boundaries – along trade routes, watersheds, etc. – and given that most of the natural trading routes in North America are north/south, are there genuine Canadian regions? Or are Halifax, Nova Scotia and Bangor, Maine interchangeable, and is Vancouver, British Columbia simply Seattle North?

The difference is this: regionalism has continued to inform Canadian popular music in a way that has largely been lost in that of the US. The music made in Philadelphia or Houston may be predominantly of one genre or another, depending on the state of the cultural mix in the city at the time, but it will not be notably different from the music of that genre made in Los Angeles, Chicago or New York. If there are differences between, say, heavy metal from Los Angeles and heavy metal from Chicago, these will have very little to do with the region from which each emanates. The surfeit of pop music in the US, and homogeneity of the record companies and radio-programming process have removed from all but very specialized distribution outlets much of the regional flavour in US popular music.

This is not so true in the Canadian case. It would be tempting to say that the traditional philosophy of the Canadian mosaic has been friendlier to regional differences than the US melting pot. More likely, Canadian-content regulations, requiring a certain percentage of domestic music in radio programming, have meant that musicians who have not had the edges rounded off of their regional backgrounds make it to Canadian airwaves. The history of Canadian culture is also inextricably linked to the advantage of having a state-owned broadcasting system, the CBC, with a mandate to promote regionalism on both radio and TV. To some extent, this has meant that artists in Canada, while they do not become stars and rarely become wealthy, nevertheless do get heard.

Let us take as an example – and an outstanding one at that – the experience of Canadian songwriter and singer Stan Rogers. Rogers' rich baritone, his social activism, and his Maritime resonances, meant that he has received exposure on Canadian airways in a way that is unlikely to have happened in the US, where even established, similar artists like Pete Seeger are very rarely heard, outside of the most specialized programs or tributes. Even on television, regional music has had a strong place at the CBC. Don Messer of *Don Messer's Jubilee*, a national television show that ran in the 1950s and 1960s, became a national voice originating in the Maritimes, and there were certainly strong folk and rural roots in that music. But that music belongs to another time.

For most of its brief, thirty-year history, rock music has been only incidentally Canadian, even when some of the best of it was being made by Canadians. But, when Burton Cummings and the Guess Who addressed the issue head-on in the early seventies, in 'American Woman', the sound and impact were at heart America. (It is interesting that Cummings' band-mate in the Guess Who, Randy Bachman, attained what is, in my view, a more remote or un-American pop sound with his next band, Bachman Turner Overdrive, and particularly with their jazz-influenced 'Blue Collar' and anthemic 'Taking Care of Business' – the latter being remade much later by a Vancouver band, DOA, as a vehicle for a music video featuring a frantic hockey match.)

More notably remote, and more influential, are Joni Mitchell and Neil Young. I have a feeling that if I were from the west, I would have a better feel for whatever regionalism has existed in Mitchell's music, but admit I have difficulty knowing whether I'm in Vancouver or Seattle. 'Here' is 'west', not Canada or the US. However, there is a gentle perception in Mitchell's music, and, once again, that recurring jazzlike feel, which I believe is related to a sense of apartness, of not being part of the pop mainstream. Her early years in Saskatchewan must have something to do with that. Mitchell's swooping vocalizations and arrythmic jazz tendencies have surfaced in the music of a a younger Torontonian, Jane Siberry. While Siberry uses reductionist technique to give her lyrics a kind of primitive or naive flair, set against a fairly sophisticated musical texture, it isn't spun like something you'd hear on a New York psychiatrist's couch: the images are often rural or domestic.

Whatever the case to be made for Mitchell's Canadianisms, I feel more comfortable doing the same for Neil Young, even though, like Mitchell, he is clearly and permanently transplanted to California. Young's estrangement from his Toronto sportscaster father was probably the most indelible of his Canadian experiences. Nevertheless, Young continues to put out classic rock and roll that is rooted in many of the same folk tendencies as that of Mitchell – strong structures, an emphasis on lyrics even in the heaviest of tunes, the use of the guitar as basis for rhythm and melody. These elements provide a direct link to the Riverboat folk club on Yorkville Avenue in Toronto.

It is no coincidence that a folk scene like that of New York in the early sixties surfaced only months later in the Yorkville folk scene in Toronto. In part, this followed a political movement, in that US draft resisters found Toronto a friendly and familiar safe haven. With only five hundred miles separating Toronto from New York – a day's hitchhike at most – Torontonians were familiar with the Bleeker Street folk scene. Canadians such as Ian and Sylvia Tyson or Gordon Lightfoot were therefore part of a folk tradition with New York roots.

Of course, the fact that folk music is essentially based on the acoustic guitar was a key ingredient shaping the 'ruralness' of its sound. This meant that the instrument most favoured in composition was available to the junior songwriter with limited means and lengthy distances between band-mates. Folk was essentially a solitary medium, and nothing better suited the rural spaces of Canada.

An essay about regional voices within Canadian popular music must say something about the music of Quebec, but the French-language tradition falls outside my main argument here – that, in desperately trying to find a voice different from those of its British parents or US cousins, English-Canadian music gave expression to its regional peculiarities. I have heard the same process at work in the way in which French-language Canadian music has borrowed heavily from other immigrant musics within North America – most notably the Celtic and Gaelic musics of the Irish and the Scots – but this would require another paper. For our purposes, we'll stick to the theme of English-Canadian regionalism, although our overview would be incomplete without discussion of at least one seminal, Quebec-based artist, Leonard Cohen.

Like novelist Mordecai Richler, Cohen's region and tradition were those of the vibrant Montreal Jewish community. A respected poet and novelist in the early 1960s, Cohen was impressed by the success of Dylan's tantalizingly obscure lyrics, rudimentary chording and instrumentation, and peculiar vocal stylings, and decided that the mid-sixties presented one of those peculiar opportunities, which occur from time to time, for the setting of poetry to music. Unlike Dylan, Cohen cannot sing, but his drone is infectious, like waking up to a truck outside your window on a subzero Montreal morning, the engine trying hard to turn over, the lethargic motor grinding ceaselessly. At other times, one can hear strains of the Hebrew cantor, or the growl of Greenwich Village bohemians of the Kerouac/Kesey eras. Early classics like 'Suzanne', with its love-generation morality and psychedelic amoebalike colours now seem dated. The later songs, like 'First We'll Take Manhattan' are more pointed, lonely, acerbic and timely. While Cohen borrowed heavily from Dylan and others of the New York rock intelligentsia, especially the Velvet Underground, his voice remains a distinctly regional Canadian one, the region of its emergence being the Montreal Jewish community. It is interesting to speculate as to how much Cohen's approach has influenced the sound of Toronto's Cowboy Junkies, whose style offers much of the same slow, deliberate, reductionist dirge and drone.

So much has been written about Gordon Lightfoot's 'Canadianness' that it may be taken as given. He is important to this argument for two reasons: his is a recognizably Canadian voice, and he didn't move to Los Angeles. Furthermore, Lightfoot offers a key to understanding why so much Canadian music has been received in the United States as country music. After his twelve-string guitar period of the 1960s, Lightfoot introduced a slide steel guitar into the mix; to the restrictive mind of the radio programmer, that signalled the sound of country music. Much of his later work – 'Daylight Katie', 'Alberta Bound', etc. – appeared mainly on country charts. Lightfoot has always had a clear sense of place and is not

embarrassed to strut it lyrically. The move to country may also be seen in the music of Murray McLaughlan, who revitalized a sagging career by going country when his rock albums did not sell. This transition illustrates one of the central themes of my argument: that country-flavoured pop is essentially Canadian pop music.

Bruce Cockburn is likewise an acoustic/folk Canadian artist with an international reputation, although he is more respected in places like Japan and Europe than in the United States. His anti-American politics, which he proclaims loudly, are no doubt to blame for this. You cannot decry US involvement in Central America and expect to get a lot of US airplay. Cockburn is another performer who is not hesitant to talk about place in his lyrics.

The long-defunct but perpetually influential Canadian group The Band took the music of the folk scene and soaked it in Arkansas rock. While The Band was originally assembled to support Ronnie Hawkins – the Svengali of Canadian rock music, himself a transplanted Arkansas Elvis clone – distinctive Canadian voices soon emerged within it. Four of the band were from southern Ontario, and brought with them an eclectic mix of regional sounds of the 1950s. Keyboardist Garth Hudson carried with him the influence of small-town church organ music. Robbie Robertson, lead guitarist and writer, who joined up with Hawkins as a roadie, had grown up on the Mohawk Six Nations reserve near Brantford. The other two members were Toronto session players, Richard Manuel and Rick Danko. Transplanted just over the border to Woodstock, New York, as house band for a recuperating Bob Dylan (fresh from a tumble off his Triumph Bonneville), The Band began to work on a very distinctive sound based around Robertson's poetic lyrics and unusual chord structures. This band sounded like no other, in part because of the remote voice they brought with them. Helm's voice, no doubt, might be associated with that of Dixie rebels – a lost, but authentic American voice that was no longer part of the mainstream, and one with curious affinities to a rural Canadian experience. Listen carefully, though, to songs like 'Whispering Pines' ('Drifting in a daze/when evenings will be done/try looking through a haze/at an empty house in the cold, cold sun') or, more pointedly, 'Acadian Driftwood', a song about the expulsion of French Acadians from Nova Scotia which nicely marries the Québécois fiddle to the Cajun music of New Orleans and contains the lyric 'I've got winter in my blood'. Even after a long hiatus, Robertson's recent solo work has tended to centre on his aboriginal roots, and, despite the claims of aboriginal politics as to the meaningless of white borders, I would still argue that this voice is essentially remote and rural and, therefore, traceable to Canadian regional influences.

As The Band expired in the mid-seventies, another kind of Canadian music was making money in the US. Loverboy, The Spoons, Honeymoon Suite and Saga were bona-fide rock stars. In contrast to The Band, however, these people had no Canadian voice at all; they were made to fit the US formula. Since there was nothing distinctive about them, they made it big in Canada only after being confirmed as authentic by our US cousins, thereby proving the cliché that 'Canada eats its young' and will listen to nothing not sanctioned by the US. That these bands were posing as American rock stars soon became as obvious to the Canadian fan as a faked injury in a National Hockey League game. Soon, and appropriately, these bands withered away.

The holy grail of a US chart hit no longer possessed hip appeal; it was seen as crass. The success of independent groups and record companies in the US and UK showed us another route. Canada went underground. We gave ourselves the luxury of time, shielded ourselves from *Billboard* bullets, and looked for what felt to be right and ours, not theirs. In other words, we tried to find out 'where is here'. Musicians stayed in their basements longer. Developing a hometown audience took on new importance. Groups like The Northern Pikes from Saskatchewan, The Grapes of Wrath from Vancouver and Blue Rodeo from Toronto stole power back from the multinational record companies and put it back in the hands of the fans. In a desperate bid to stay hip, record companies drove down to the artsy warehouse district to sign bands, in an effort to capitalize on the underground swell. Canadian music benefited. People who deserved record deals got them, since they had usually already released their own product independently and perhaps even had a video. They were better rehearsed, and more likely to achieve what they wanted, musically. The sound was different, and more like our own.

The self-consciousness of US-clonelike Loverboy rock was gone, replaced by a new confidence. The hip quotient came from not being from somewhere else, from the satisfaction of a joke that middle America couldn't get. In the face of this positive underground attitude, punk didn't survive well in Canada. Its tunelessness was somehow imported, and there were no genuine street politics to go along with it. Useful bands, such as Rough Trade, attempted to capitalize on the existence of an increasingly politicized gay and lesbian audience, and produced some fine music in the process, but, predictably, found no commercial backing.

Meanwhile, back on Queen Street, the heart of Toronto's downtown music scene, the new voices included that of Handsome Ned, who led a kind of urban country band, and whose death of a heroine overdose became a key moment in the marshalling of a 'cow-punk' community. Many clubs ended their aimless association with punk and 'New Music' and returned to a more focused, country-oriented policy. Among the most influential of the groups to emerge from this scene is Blue Rodeo, who combine the exceptional musical talents of Greg Keillor with the voice of Jim Cuddy, and have achieved real commercial success – including AM radio play – with such heavily country-flavoured songs as 'Try'. Keillor's understanding of the rich chordal advantage of the guitar-based melody and the country hiccup in Cuddy's strong voice provide a perfect crossover mix. Even Keillor's own Dylanlike voice, on a song like 'Diamond Mine', remains rooted in the *Nashville Skyline* era of strong melodies. The Toronto band Prairie Oyster is also on the cusp of success, helping Nashville to rediscover early 1950s-style country music.

The other notable voice to have emerged over the past five years in Toronto is that of women singers, who offer a different sensibility easily accommodated within the country form. The Cowboy Junkies provide, perhaps, the best example. Highlighting singer Margo Timmins' mournful voice, the Cowboy Junkies first achieved cult status, and, subsequently, more popular acceptance with their valium-laced approach. Musically infantile arrangements did not diminish their impact, since they were tapping into the kind of languid melancholy that country music has always provided. If you listen to Timmins' a-cappella version of 'Mining for Gold' on their *Trinity Sessions* album, however, the hipness of country hurt becomes very evident. The Junkies' debt to the style of Leonard Cohen has already been mentioned.

Less prominent but still relevant to this argument, is Mary Margaret O'Hara, who, in order to get a recording deal, had to go to the UK, where her debut album *Miss America* was a critical success. O'Hara has had a long history in Toronto bands, moving from Songship in the late 1970s through the Go Deo Chorus in the early 1980s to her recent solo career. O'Hara's long auburn hair, her scattered, erratic style and washer-woman dresses make her a queen of ultra-hip gloss on Sissy Spacek-as-Loretta-Lynn. Nevertheless, O'Hara's hiccupy voice can belt out a song with force, and, on a barn-burner like 'Brand New Day' on her debut album, the country influence is strong and unmistakable.

No other woman – indeed, perhaps, no other performer – has done more in the past five years for the mainstreaming of country music than k. d. lang, whose widely acclaimed voice has deservedly met with success in the United States. Lang cannot be considered a Toronto artist, despite the time she has spent in that city, but she has set the standards for Toronto performers. The recipient of many industry awards in both Canada and the US, lang came into real commercial prominence after 'Crying', her duet with the late Roy Orbison. Lang is one of the few pop singers capable of matching Orbison's own vocal range; following Orbison's recent death, her rendering of that song as a tribute of sorts won her many fans. No amount of professionalism could imbue lang's rendering with that much emotion if it was not heartfelt. In six short years, lang has swung from a kind of goofy, galumphing style to a very sophisticated and highly individual one. Her politics, nevertheless, may impede her progress – her outspoken stand against eating meat has not won her many favours from middle-American radio stations.

Many other names might be included here to demonstrate the turn of Canadian popular music towards country music – and a female country music at that. At the same time, an earlier generation of country singers is maintaining a strong following. Ian Tyson's authentically cowboyish approach to singing remains a true regional voice of the west. Even Stompin' Tom Connors, with his broadly nationalistic songs about quintessentially Canadian characters, has ended a ten-year hiatus – during which he thumbed his nose at the Canadian recording industry – with two sold-out shows at Toronto's Massey Hall in the fall of 1990.

Having demonstrated the existence of this trend, we might well ask what are its implications. Country music is, after all, essentially American, a borrowed form. Why, then, have young Canadians, particularly young urban

Canadians, adopted it as their own, and with what do they infuse it that the Americans do not?

One of the attractions of country music as a form is the extent to which it is unashamed of its emotional rawness. Between periods of sophistication (Hank Williams, Sr., and some more recent artists) there flourished an awful lot of hurtin' housewife music. The main attraction of that music was how personal the blond-bouffanted singers could be concerning their lives; this was sung gossip, its themes those of the 'loved, abused and left'. Women were appendages, and happy to cast themselves that way. As a result, that music became irrelevant to feminist and postfeminist audiences. The new country music has jettisoned that point of view, and replaced it with one which is much more ironic and relevant. A second major source of the form's attraction is that it is musically simple, and, therefore, broadly accessible to both players and audiences. The danger of this simplicity is that it can leave a bad band with less to hide behind – less instrumentation, less volume and less density.

Canadian country music has a twang to it, but that twang is not the authoritative southern drawl; rather, it reflects the dropped 'g's and plain irony of the Canadian concession roads. If this is the Canadian voice, how is it heard, particularly in the vast, yawning market to the south, the home of country music?

In many ways, that voice has important connections to US country music. Linguists have argued that the closest accent to that of lower-class seventeenth-century English speech is perhaps to be found in the Appalachian hills, where early English settlers to Virginia moved shortly after their arrival on this side of the big pond and lived in isolation, holding that accent in time. That hillbilly accent, of course, has passed from bluegrass folksongs to the country music of today. Can the same be argued for the snowbound villages along the 49th parallel north of the border? Basically, no – the Canadian experience is primarily a technological one, in that it only really began after lines of communication and transportation were well developed. Since these Canadian villages were always situated so as to serve the railroad, the isolation was more perceived than real.

The way in which the Canadian voice is heard in the US market is nevertheless dependent upon another, more important factor. To understand it, we should turn for a minute to a relationship between two other countries in the early part of this century, one which parallels that of Canada to the US. Those countries are Ireland and England. Between 1890 and 1930, much of the world's best English-language literature was not written in England, but in Ireland, or, at the very least, by Irish writers. Consider the list: Oscar Wilde, Bernard Shaw, W. B. Yeats, James Joyce, Sean O'Casey, Sam Beckett. This happened after two centuries of British political, cultural and economic imperialism of the worst order, and a foreign policy that bordered at one point on genocide. At the end of that terrible period, Irish writers were setting literary standards. Why?

Put simply, this occurred because, during that forty-year period of history, the Irish voice attained a critical mass. That voice was from a country that spoke English extraordinarily well (after its own language was banned), but it was at the same time a very different one: it was, first of all, a Catholic voice, but also mystical, nationalistic and angry. From Shaw's wordy journalistic commentary on British morality to Wilde's cutting satire of English society, to Yeats' nationalism, to O'Casey's voice of the lower-class Dubliner and Joyce's globally comic re-creation of Dublin from exile – all of these depend on a perspective that is non-English, and yet *in* English (or, in Joyce's case, in a *kind* of English).

And so it is, or will be soon, with the Canadian voice. Canadians have been dominated by successive imperial influences: by the British before World War II, by the US since then. As we approach the end of this century, the Canadian voice will achieve, from within our own unique and removed perspective, an authority and critical mass. What, then, of Canada's French province, Quebec? Its remoteness, from the perspective of the US audience, is clear. In many respects, Quebec is far ahead of English Canada in the quest for self-realization, and its singers have often been politically radical. In part because they believe that their culture will continue to be consumed at home, the Québécois seem unthreatened by Canada's Free Trade Agreement with the US, even though, disappointingly, much of their own popular music is in English.

Like any industrial or economic commodity in Canada, the business of music follows natural trading lines. The natural linkages, for Canadian music and most other commercial goods, are north-south rather than east-west. But this is nothing new. The first immigrant Canadians knew that the only way to battle that geographic reality was to carve a railway through the north-south barriers and create an artificial country of whistlestop towns along the US border. While political boundaries have always been essentially artificial, they may be defended. Airwaves cannot. As a result, Canadians tended to listen to US radio stations.

Nevertheless, that situation has produced its own backlash. The sheer artificiality of Canada as a notional country has produced within it a constant search for identity, a creativity focused on the question of 'Where is Here?' That identity, of course, is easier to define negatively, as what it is not; and what it has not been, since 1980 or so, is American. In the 1950s, people knew what hockey announcer Foster Hewitt meant when he opened every *Hockey Night in Canada* broadcast with 'Hello Canada and hockey fans in the United States'. What he meant was this: 'All Canada is of course listening to this hockey game, and a few sturdy souls in the soulless US probably have enough good sense to come to appreciate this northern game too.' Canadian music in the 1980s finally possessed enough momentum to make its crucial breakaway.

To return, though, to economic links: these have always been anti-Canadian for geographical reasons, and have now been rendered anti-Canadian by the official free-trade policy of the Canadian government. Large multinational record companies will be unlikely to see Toronto as the regional headquarters of the north-east or central midwest. We will simply be commercial outposts within the vast suburban US market. Paradoxically,

I think that could be quite good for Canadian music which, in the 1990s, will rely less and less on US multinationals for either production or distribution. While awaiting substantial sales in the North American market, Canadian music will achieve cult status, and that status has always been accorded good music on the leading edge. Being taken off the 'A' list for US distribution will have the salutary effect of making fewer Canadian rock stars rich, but it may render Canadian popular music of genuine regional value. Ironically, this may prove of interest to a US audience, if Canadian music attains the status held by Australian films today or Irish literature in the early part of this century.

In the effort to engender a feeling of national unity, Canada has had to go to extreme measures: a national railroad, a national radio and television service, Canadian-content quotas. But the railroads sit rusting and free trade may erode many of our cultural institutions. Still, it is precisely at this precarious moment that Canadian music will find its true voice. A new confidence, gained from international recognition on our own terms, will be the start of a new movement in Canadian music. 'Here' is where we are, and we like it. We know what we're not, and we're not 'There'.

As Canadians lose faith in the ability of their politicians to pull a country together from the mess of the Meech Lake Accord (an attempt to finally include Quebec in our Constitution, which turned into a political fiasco), they naturally turn to other ways of identifying and valorizing themselves. Whether you're sitting on the docks in Lunenberg, Nova Scotia waiting for the boats to come in from the Grand Banks of Newfoundland or driving through the foothills of the Rocky Mountains in a half-ton truck looking for stray steer, the music on the truck radios will be country music. Outside Toronto, country music is everywhere, and, even in Toronto, it's available on two radio stations all the time.

Urban country music is the sound of Toronto recognizing that it is merely the place where people from across Canada have gathered to make money. Country music is a maturing form, and one to which large numbers of people turn to hear resonances of where they came from, blended with the cosmopolitanism of where they are now. It is a commentary on the US form, and, in many cases, has improved upon that form and will take it in new directions for years to come.

In this sad moment of our national history, with the country directionless and adrift, Canadians are now turning to the one shred of identity remaining – and that identity is found in the arts. Even some in the government have realized that the only hope for pulling this country back together again lies in our collective vision of ourselves as expressed in the arts. The newly founded 'Citizens' Forum on Canada's Future' wants our destiny articulated by poets rather than politicians and lawyers. I would call that real progress. Our new national identity will be built on a strong base, and a maturing regional voice will be there to sing it out. As remote as our songs may have been, they are getting close to the heart of things and it is at the heart of things that country music is most often found.

Notes

1 This article is an excerpt from my book *Success Without College*, forthcoming from Penguin Books Canada Ltd. The title refers to Northrop Frye's *The Bush Garden* (Toronto: Anansi, 1971). See also Frye's *Divisions on a Ground* (Toronto: Anansi, 1982).
2 Laurie's manuscript uses the terms 'CanLit', 'CanPop' and 'CanCult', familiar to many Canadians. In the interests of international understanding, I have changed these to their fuller forms, but I wished to signal, in a note, the author's use of these more suggestive abbreviations (Will Straw).

Laurie Brown is an arts journalist for CBC television and reports on the program The Journal *seen nation wide*

LAWRENCE GROSSBERG

ROCK, TERRITORIALIZATION AND POWER[1]

Most discussions of the politics of contemporary rock (using rock in its broadest possible sense) start by assuming that, in some sense, rock has lost its political edge. In its most sophisticated forms, such an argument is not intended merely to say that rock has become establishment culture or that it has been colonized by corporate interests (both of which may be true to some extent). Instead, it points to the doubly paradoxical situation of contemporary popular music. First, there seems to be an enormous amount of political activity within rock culture (especially on the side of the musicians) and some very real efforts to explicitly reconnect rock to a sense of political activisim. And yet, these activities (whether in terms of lyrics, organizational identifications through such activities as concerts, or direct political involvement) seem to have almost no impact upon either rock audiences or the broader tendencies of rock culture.

Second, given that rock seems totally incapable of organizing any significant politically oppositional force at the moment, it does seem odd that there is so much energy being directed against it. These attacks have taken a number of different, even contradictory forms: the effort to ban rock music entirely (e.g., the Christian fundamentalist rejection of all rock as the devil's work and Allen Bloom's attempt to blame rock culture for the failure of American values); the effort to regulate and discipline rock music by placing the authority to judge and discriminate between good and bad music in external – the state and family – authorities (e.g., the Parents Music Resource Center and the various civil and criminal prosecutions of rock groups); and finally the effort to rearticulate the very meaning and possibilities of rock's social position (e.g., Lee Atwater as a rock star, or Pat Boone's statement that he deserves to be in the Rock and Roll Hall of Fame for having made rock 'nice').

In order to begin to make sense of these paradoxes, we need a better sense of where the politics of rock are located, of the possibilities of and constraints on its articulations. Rock has had a variety of political positions, powers and effects since its emergence in the early to mid-1950s. Sometimes its politics have involved the organization of individual experience, or the configurations of everyday life, or the structure of social relationships and differences, or even, on rare occasions, the explicit distribution of political and economic power. The history of rock can be seen to involve a series of interrupted struggles to articulate (or disarticulate) particular sounds, texts, genres and styles, to specific meaning, social positions and ideologies and, from there, to specific political positions and effects, or to the 'necessary absence' of politics at a particular conjuncture. But unless we begin by acknowledging the constraints and limits operating on the articulation of rock to politics, we are likely to fall back into a naively romantic view which simply assumes that rock was and is supposed to be resistant and/or oppositional.

I want to suggest that, given the conditions of possibility which both called forth and enabled rock's existence as an articulation of musical, cultural, economic and technological practices, it is simply mistaken to assume that rock was, in any significant way, outside of the political mainstream of American culture. Consider the political, social and economic climate of the post-war United States (one set of the conditions of possibility for rock's emergence): an unstable and unequally distributed economic prosperity and optimism; the conversion of the productive apparatus to consumerist goals; a corporate compromise between labor and capital mediated by the state (committed to extending civil liberties in order to expand the consumer population); and most importantly, a peculiar version of liberalism ('the end of ideology') built upon a precarious balance between a sense that difference mattered culturally and socially but not politically (i.e., it was no longer a disruptive or oppositional force).

The result was a powerful context of mobility and change, both in terms of images and experiences. But there was a particular image of the proper and possible form of mobility: ameliorism in both social and economic terms. This was a gradual process which had to be earned and which, when successfully completed, would reproduce the unity of the political consensus in the image of the social and cultural mainstream. America would create, not only the first politically liberal society but also the first society which had created its own middle-class style as the consensual norm of everyday life. Of course, this mobility was counterbalanced by a very real quietism or conservatism which pervaded every aspect of the nation's life. It was against the image of this social conservativism that the romantic vision of rock as an inherent statement of political resistance or, at least, an expression of alienation, was formed. This then quickly became the necessary condition of 'authenticity' in rock culture.

I want, instead, to emphasize the ways this context constrained the political possibilities of rock so that it was difficult, if not impossible, for rock to enter into any explicit ideological struggle or political resistance. Rock did not challenge the ideological consensus of American life but it did attempt to escape the quietism of culture and everyday life. This has in fact always been the limits of rock's politics. Perhaps a part of the reason that the romantic version of rock's political agenda won out was the assumed identification of rock with a particular image: the rocker as the isolated and agonized rebel and delinquent, antisocial, antidomestic and anticonsumerist. This is, of course, an inaccurate portrait, not only of the majority of rock fans but of the performers as well.

There is little evidence – even in the songs – that rock rejected the dominant consensus of American society, or its major ideological assumptions, including sexism, racism and classism. It is not merely that most fans lived somewhere inside the vast center of American society, it is also that they imagined themselves remaining within it (or even, moving more toward the center insofar as it defined the middle-class image of success). This is not to claim that rock fans wanted to grow up living the same lives as their parents, but then what generation does. They assumed that the center would change but their imagination of such changes was itself defined by the ameliorism of the dominant consensus. Nowhere in this was there any room for ideological questions. Rock's politics were firmly located within the commitment to mobility and consumerism, perhaps not as ends in themselves but as the necessary conditions for a life of fun. That is, rock culture never renounced the normative passion for comfort and success. Because they were caught in the space between the discipline and boredom of the school and the family (the two dominant sites of youth's policing), rock fans used rock to imagine their own space of enjoyment, pleasure and fun, a space regulated only by the norms of the rock culture itself. But this space was not a replacement for school or family (although it may have suggested the possibility of less rigid organizations for these institutions). Being a rock fan certainly did not entail, and only rarely involved even imagining, the possibility of leaving school – it remained the necessary path to secure the consumerist lifestyle and its associated pleasures – or renouncing family and a domestic future.

Rock did not reject the domestic image of daily life, including the privileged position it gave to men in both gender and sexual relations. While rock, as well as the image of the rocker, were often positioned outside the family, the vast majority of songs and fans reproduced the desire for love and the stable relationships of the nuclear family. While rock did create a space in which women's sexuality and pleasure were publically legitimated, it was often romanticized and almost always defined in relation to the male partner, viewer or listener. This does not deny that the sexual power of rock music, performance and dance were new to its fans, nor that it was seen, by its fans but even more by the mainstream population, as a rupture in, even a threat to, the quiet regulation of sensuality and sexuality.

Similarly, the dominant class politics remained largely in place, reinflected only through romantic fantasies of different class experiences, and of the possibilities which these implied for the members of each class to escape the structures of control and discipline of their own class. So too regarding race relations, rock was firmly located within the ambiguity of the dominant consensus: both ameliorist and racist, rock's relations to Black music, performers and audiences has always been a highly selective one. The apparent absence of a gap between Black and white music and musical taste in the 1950s – a gap which has been constantly reinscribed since then – says more about the organization of the economics of distribution (limited repertoires of available musics, limited number of venues for peformance, etc.) than it does about the politics of the rock culture itself. Again, this does not deny that rock – performers, performances and fans – did position itself significantly further along the ameliorist ladder of improved race relations. But it did not challenge the taken-for-granted terms of the ideologically and institutionally constructed racism of the US, and it most certainly did not offer any critique of the dominant ideology.

Yet once again, to the extent that this was seen – not by rock fans as much as by the mainstream adult culture – as having allowed the interracial mobility implicit in the rhetoric of the liberal consensus to be accomplished more quickly than their racism desired, rock was seen as something of a political challenge. Thus, it was precisely because rock so innocently accepted its place within the liberal consensus that it was so easily embroiled in and articulated to political struggles, but always by others. Thus, I am not claiming that rock did not challenge, upset, distance itself from, the dominant social systems of power and discipline. I am claiming that rock's challenge was rarely articulated by or from within the rock culture itself but always by those outside of, and to some extent, opposed to it. I am also claiming that, while rock sought to rock the cultural boat (quietism), it did so with little or no concern for the organization of political consensus and economic relations since it did not consider that these were connected to questions of culture and fun. Rock sought to open culture to the needs and experiences of its own audiences, not to deny or overturn the consensual and institutional structures which had made those experiences, and rock's existence, possible. Its politicization resulted primarily from the sustained attacks it elicited rather than from its own activities or intentions. Perhaps those who opposed rock recognized that it was not quiet, aesthetically, culturally or socially; perhaps they were afraid that its attempt to upset the consensual economy of cultural taste and pleasure would have wider ramifications. In any case, the result was that the rock formation often found itself articulated outside of the very consensus in which it still located itself. We might say that rock was politicized 'behind its back'. In its effort to fight back against its own expulsion from the mainstream, rock did sometimes politicize itself further. And this was not always only the result of its attempts to protect itself. Nor was it merely because it occasionally realized that it wanted to fight for the very things for which it was being attacked; it was just as often because it was exciting, if not fun, to be placed – temporarily at least – in the position of troublemaker. It was a way for youth to assert its own place. Ultimately, rock's distance from the mainstream, and its dissonant voice within it, was the result of the way rock mattered to its fans, and of the things that it made matter as well.

Almost four decades later, everything has changed. The political, social and economic climate is radically different. The economic boom is over; the optimism is gone; the corporate compromise is rapidly being whittled away. While mobility is still the dominant social norm, it has an entirely different face: it is defined in purely economic (monetary and consumerist) terms with no sense of a common social class being created; it is instantaneous and it does not require labor or merit. Finally, difference has returned with a vengeance; it is omnipresent, dangerous and yet glamorous. Certainly there are those who would use this changing historical context to explain the two paradoxes referred to above: that it is increasingly difficult to see how rock can be articulated to political positions and struggles and, at the same time, rock is under increasing attack.

But this response is, in the end, too easy, for it ignores two fundamental aspects of rock music and culture, aspects which may help us understand why it so important to challenge rock's privileged status without rejecting it altogether. First, we need to remind ourselves that rock is a form of music – and while this is quite obvious, discussions of rock often miss the unique relation of music and power. Second, the specificity of rock as a form of popular culture depends upon its special relation to everyday life, a relation that makes it particularly important in the current political context.

In order to understand music's specific relation to power, we must come to terms with music's specific power. But in a society (and a history) driven to master the power of the word, and mastered by that power, it is difficult, to say the least, to describe the apparently immediate and almost mystical (because, to some extent, universal) relationship that music constitutes, both between itself and its audience, and between its audience and their environment. By describing it as 'almost mystical', I mean to register the necessary uncertainty that we must have about the social determination of music's power (remembering its use in ritual and religion), while at the same time acknowledging that the actual historical forms of music are always socially determined. Jacques Attali has described music as 'a herald, for change is inscribed in noise faster than it transforms society' (1985: 5). And later, he expands upon this: music 'makes audible the new world that will gradually become visible, that will impose itself and regulate the order of things; it is not only the image of things, but the transcending of the everyday' (11). (I will return to the last phrase shortly.) For Attali then, one can read changes in musical form, in the dominant and emergent codes organizing their production and consumption, as 'prophesy' of the political transformations looming ahead in society's future. For Attali, there is always a correspondence, somewhere displaced, between the technologies of musical production, the codes of music's regularity, and the political economy of the social formation. (In fact, he identifies four moments of such correspondence: sacrifice, representation, repetition and composition.) But I am less concerned here with such structural relations than with Attali's recognition that '[l]istening to music is listening to all noise, realizing that its appropriation and control is a reflection of power, that it is essentially political. . . . And since noise is the source of power, power has always listened to it with fascination' (6).

What does it mean to say that 'noise' or, more to the point, music 'is the source of power'? For if we can understand this relation, then we should have no trouble understanding why power would find it necessary to appropriate and control it. Attali is, I believe, too romantic when he writes, 'Rumblings of revolution. Sounds of competing powers. Clashing noises, of which the musician is the mysterious, strange, and ambiguous forerunner – after having been long emprisoned, a captive of power. . . . But a subversive strain of music has always managed to survive, subterranean and pursued, the inverse image of this political channelisation: Popular music, an instrument of the ecstatic cult, an outburst of uncensored violence' (12–13). I should perhaps add, at this point, that Attali does not see rock as popular music: 'From Jazz to Rock. Continuations of the same effort, always resumed and renewed, to alienate a liberatory will in order to produce a market, that is, supply and demand at the same time' (103). Rather than follow Attali into this zero sum game in which we must constantly seek to discriminate between the co-opted and the subversive text, I prefer to take my lead from a more direct, if somewhat more naive, statement he makes: 'Ambiguous and fragile, ostensibly secondary and of minor importance, [music] has invaded our world and daily life. Today, it is unavoidable, as if, in a world now devoid of meaning, a background noise were increasingly necessary to give people a sense of security' (3). We need only think of the image of the mother singing to her child!

But how does music give people a sense of security? To say that the answer has to do with music's enormous and, to a large extent, inexplicable ability to 'move' or stir people is too vapid an understatement, for it treats music's power in purely figurative terms. Obviously, it is true that music somehow calls people emotionally. But it is perhaps better to begin by acknowledging the insight in Carlos Mejia Godoy's explanation of why the contras would inevitably lose in Nicaragua: 'They have no singers. . . . We have singers.' Would it not then be more accurate to say that music is the most powerful affective agency in human life; music seems, almost independently of our intentions, to produce and orchestrate our moods, both qualitatively and quantitatively. Here one need only think of the impact of background and soundtrack musics, whether in media texts (e.g., the differences between the use of music in *Miami Vice* and *Twin Peaks*) or in the places of everyday activities (e.g., muzak). Behind these diverse uses of music is the implicit recognition that, somehow, such musical environments strongly influence the rhythms, tempos and intensities of our lives. They can in fact determine the sorts of investments we make and the activities we undertake in their musically constructed spaces. We might turn, for an image of this power, to Deleuze and Guattari's 'refrain' of creation, made manifest in the construction of the musical refrain itself:

> A child in the dark, gripped with fear, comforts himself by singing under his breath. He walks and halts to his song. Lost, he takes shelter, or orients himself with his little song as best he can. The song is like a rough sketch of a calming and stabilizing, calm and stable, center in the heart of chaos. . . . Now we are at home. But home does not preexist: it was necessary to draw a circle around that uncertain and fragile center, to organize a limited space. Many, very diverse, components have a part in this, landmarks and marks of all kinds. . . . Sonorous or vocal components are very important: a wall of sound, or at least a wall with some sonic bricks in it. A child hums to summon the strength for the schoolwork she has to hand in. A housewife sings to herself, or listens to the radio, as she

marshals the antichaos forces of her work. Radios and television sets are like sound walls around every household and mark territories (the neighbor complains when it gets too loud). For sublime deeds like the foundation of a city or the fabrication of a golem, one draws a circle, or better yet walks in a circle as in a children's dance, combining rhythmic vowels and consonants ... A mistake in speed, rhythm, or harmony would be catastrophic because it would bring back the forces of chaos, destroying both creator and creation. (1987: 311)

Deleuze and Guattari are here attributing to music an enormous territorializing power. In my own terms, it is music which founds place. It is music which calls forth our investments and hence, our affective anchors into reality. It is music which affectively locates us in the world by constructing the rhythms of our stopping and going. When we stop, when the music enables us to stop, we ourselves are positioned, not by an already existing stable identity, but by the wall which our music (our affect) constructs around a bit of space. We are protected now to engage in whatever activities are necessary, and enabled to move on in ways that were not possible before, since the wall reconstructs the space outside just as surely as it constitutes a place inside. Everyday life is itself organized by the rhythms of places and spaces, and by the specific configurations of places. This is merely to say that music, or more specifically, rock culture, organizes the mattering maps by which everyday life becomes navigable and hence, liveable.

But there seems to be a contradiction here: for at another point in their work, Deleuze and Guattari refer to music as the most 'deterritorializing' of all practices; they claim that music destroys the codes which guarantee the repeatability necessary to both power and everyday life. How are we to bring these two notions together? How are we to make sense of the claim that music is a primary agency of both territorializing and deterritorializing forces? But isn't that just what rhythm is about? Is that not the very function of rhythm: to regulate the relations of place and space, of territorializing and deterritorializing. Meaghan Morris has pointed to a different image of everyday life as travel in the creation myth cited above. In this image, contrary to Western common sense (in which one leaves a home already established to travel to some other home), mobility precedes and is more basic than, stability. Space then takes precedence over place.

We begin with a necessary contradiction: territorializing and deterritorializing. And yet somehow, the story we tell always seems to put the former into the service of the latter. Place in the service of space, stability in the service of mobility. Attali has described the same perplexing situation at a different level of abstraction, one to which I referred above and to which we shall have to return: 'No organized society can exist without structuring differences at its core. No market economy can develop without erasing those differences in mass production' (1985: 5).

The image of everyday life which Deleuze and Guattari's myth of musical creation offers might be described as a disciplined mobilization. A disciplined mobilization is a particular dynamic structuring of places and spaces, a closed circuit of everyday life. Once you have entered into its spaces, there are no longer any frontiers or boundaries to cross, for any such line would mark the possibility of a place. Instead everyday life becomes a transit compulsion in which sites of investment are transformed into epidemics which appear everywhere (and hence nowhere, as in the war on drugs) and ultimately into pure mobilities. One can only continue to move along the frontier as along a Möbius strip. There is no longer an outside or an inside, only the constant movement within the frontier itself. A disciplined mobilization signals the triumph of an unconstrained mobility which is nothing but a principle of constraint.

Perhaps then it makes sense that attacks on rock would appear at just the moment they did, when rock culture has been called back to its roots in rhythm and dance, when club rock so powerfully dominates the culture, and when, as Frith has described it, the most powerful pleasures in rock seem to be produced out of the contradictions between the central and powerful rhythms and the increasingly less memorable 'soundtrack' melodies. In fact, we might consider that punk's self-referential attack on rock helped to undermine rock's ability to establish any place. In a sense, punk transformed rock into a disciplined mobilization of sorts (and in that sense, may have unintentionally played into the hands of the contemporary forces of conservativism and capitalism). The possibility of such a close relationship between rock and this particular cultural structure makes sense when we consider the way in which youth, the audience of rock, has been constructed in the post-war US: shuttled around with no place of its own.

Perhaps this helps to make it clear why its regulation – its ownership and control – must become a priority in any struggle, like that to put into place a new conservativism, explicitly directed to the structures of everyday life itself. Consequently, the ambiguities, selectivities and differences within the new conservative's attack on rock make perfect sense if the task at hand requires the appropriation rather than the disappearance of musical relations. Music is then precisely a force that needs to be harnessed to the project of the new conservativism. But even more directly, there may be a close relationship between the specific effectivity of contemporary rock and specific project of the new conservative alliance which is, I believe, precisely to construct everyday life on the model of a disciplined mobilization. For reconstructing everyday life itself on the order of a disciplined mobilization defines a specific form of depoliticization, one-dimensionality and even narcotization. It is a socially constructed discipline of apathy built upon the very possibilities of postmodern cynicism and irony. In a disciplined mobilization, there can be no outside or, more accurately, there can be no way of connecting everyday life to the political and economic forces which are shaping it.

I want now to turn briefly to my second point: the specificity of rock culture as defined by its distinctive relationship to everyday life. This can provide further insight into the specific (different but coexistent) forms which the attacks on rock have taken, and into their combined effectivity. Attali argues that music always transcends the everyday. I would change this statement, only partly to reflect my own use of everyday life as an historically produced plane of existence which is unequally distributed. That is, I am using 'everyday life' here as a specific, historically produced form of daily life (following Lefebvre), built upon principles of repetition, redundancy (and ultimately, boredom). Its unequal distribution makes it a privilege determined largely in economic terms. Consequently, unlike Attali, I would rather say that music produced by and for a population already living in everyday life is always about the possibility of transcending the specific configuration of everyday life within which it is active. Lefebvre in fact draws a close parallel between music and everyday life: 'Music is movement, flow, time, and yet it is based on recurrence.' (1984: 19) When he asks whether music 'express[es] the secret nature of everyday life, or compensates, on the contrary, for its triviality and superficiality?' our answer must be that it does both. In fact, it is precisely in attempting to transcend particular forms of recurrence (everyday life) that music is able to express its secret nature.

Returning to my earlier discussion of rock culture, I believe that the implication of its conditions of possibility in the 1950s was that rock culture could only seek to transcend the specific configuration of everyday life, the specific forms of repetition, mundanity and triviality characterizing the everyday life in which it found itself imprisoned. That is, rock did not seek to transcend everyday life itself, to open itself out onto other planes of political, social and economic existence. It operated with and within, it took for granted, the luxury and privilege of everyday life as the condition of possibility of its own struggle against the mundanity of its everyday life. At best, rock sought to change the possibilities – the rhythms – within everyday life itself. It did not construct for itself a space outside of everyday life. (Consider the music of the Pet Shop Boys.)

Instead, it appropriated as its own the markers of places outside of everyday life which other musics, other voices had constructed. These voices and the places they marked became the signs of authenticity within the everyday life of rock culture, but they were the voices of peoples who had no everyday life, who existed outside the privileged spaces of the repetitiously mundane world of rock culture. Rock then attacked, or at least attempted to transcend, its own everyday life, its own conditions of possibility, by appropriating the images and sounds of an authenticity constituted outside of, and in part by the very absence of, everyday life.

Rock is not merely white boys singing the blues; it is the sound of those who are imprisoned within everyday life, who cannot imagine its negation (and only ambiguously desire it), trying to produce the sounds of those who have no everyday life. Consequently, rock could never address questions of politics, society or economics directly; its politics are often determined by those moments when political realities impinge upon its everyday life (e.g., the draft rather than the fact of a genocidal war being waged against the Vietnamese) or when it can be reduced to a question of everyday life (e.g., it can protest the suffering of Blacks under apartheid but it cannot acknowledge the international political economic system which sustains apartheid and a multitude of other repressive regimes). Its most powerfully resonant music comes when it acknowledges that it can only see the realities of such questions through the structures of its everyday life (e.g., the best countercultural music, and the most powerful punk music). Thus, when Simon Frith writes that 'American rock music now is a form of easy listening' (*Voice*, 24 April 1990: 91), there is a sense in which it has always been true but only now is it becoming blatantly obvious.

Rock however has a more ambiguous and ambivalent relation to everyday life and, given its power and popularity, can make a powerful ally if it can be 'appropriated and controlled', inflected into a project other than its own, unknowingly articulated into a new vector of effectivity. It can become not only a site of struggle but an agent in somebody else's struggle. But this is a very unstable task and, at the very least, it must be constantly policed, and ways must be found to ensure that it will continue to move only within the lines of the disciplined mobilization of everyday life. The struggle over rock, then, is an ongoing but specific contestation within a larger field. But the questions remain, haunting any effort to understand the struggle: whose struggle is it? what are the stakes? what can we do about it?

Note

1 This paper draws on material from my forthcoming book, *We Gotta Get Out Of This Place: Popular Conservatism and Postmodern in Contemporary America*. New York: Routledge.

References

Attali, Jacques (1985) *Noise: The Political Economy of Music*. Trans. Brian Massumi. Minneapolis: University of Minnesota Press.

Deleuze, Gilles and Guattari, Felix (1987) *A Thousand Plateaus: Capitalism and Schizophrenia*. Trans. Brian Massumi. Minneapolis: University of Minnesota Press.

Lefebvre, Henri (1984) *Everyday Life in the Modern World*. Trans. Sacha Rabinovitch. New Brunswick: Transaction.

Larry Grossberg is a co-editor of Cultural Studies *and an Associate Professor in the Unit for Criticism and Interpretation at the University of Illinois, Urbana-Champaign*

WILL STRAW

SYSTEMS OF ARTICULATION, LOGICS OF CHANGE: COMMUNITIES AND SCENES IN POPULAR MUSIC

'The Music Industry in a Changing World': concluding remarks[1]

The most welcome feature of the conference on which this *Cultural Studies* is based was the sense that issues perpetually on the agenda at meetings of popular-music scholars were being held up for re-examination. In large measure, this was dictated by the 'Changing World' of the conference's title, and in the autumn of 1990 that phrase was more resonant than usual. Global ownership trends within the cultural industries and the emergence of a unified and enlarged European market had cast doubts on the continued usefulness of such long-entrenched unities as 'Anglo-American rock', as Simon Frith's presentation suggested. A panel dealing with the relationship between popular music and the state revealed a divergence of interests between European and United States scholars, most notably around censorship and record labelling controversies and the degree to which these should be seen as central to the contemporary politics of popular music.[2]

Almost as striking, given the long-standing preoccupation of popular-music scholars with the concept of community, was the growing influence of certain tendencies within cultural theory, in particular those marked by an engagement with concepts of space and nation. The caution which has accompanied discussions of musical authenticity within popular-music studies has only recently come to be directed at notions of a regional or national musical space.[3] This is reflected, in part, in a new interest in the diversity of musical practices unfolding within particular urban centres, one of whose effects has been to undermine claims as to the uniformity of local musical cultures. Within Canadian and Québécois discussions of popular music, this same caution has been evident in critical responses to (or crises in) the politics of cultural nationalism, echoes of which were heard in conference debates over the link between music and cultural identity.

The long-standing concern of popular-music scholars with the disruption and fragmentation of cultural communities has often masked – in part through its nobility of purpose – the investment in imaginary unities which underlies it. Those encountering ethnomusicological studies for the first time after an apprenticeship in the hermeneutics of suspicion may, like myself, be struck by the prominence within them of notions of cultural totality or claims asserting the expressive unity of musical practices. Many of these premises have been maintained, albeit in a much less coherent form, in the sociology and criticism of rock music. Here, the articulatory force of specific musical practices has often displaced the integrity of cultural communities as the guarantee of music's meaningfulness, but one may still find a privileging of the geographically local as guarantee of the historical continuity of musical styles.

If the status of the local has been transformed within contemporary societies, this is in part through the workings of what Edward Said has called an 'increasingly universal system of articulation' (Said, 1990: 8). This 'system' is, obviously, shaped by economic and institutional globalization, and it is the task of a critical political economy to account for its effects. (Paul Rutten's paper, pages 292–303 in this issue, offers useful tools for doing so.) The risk remains that an emphasis on the disruptive effects of economic reordering will result in the valorization of musical practices perceived to be rooted in geographical, historical and cultural unities which are stable and conflated. Popular-music scholars and analysts of the cultural industries have generally been less attentive to ways in which this same system of articulation is produced by migrations of populations and the formation of cultural diaspora which have transformed the global circulation of cultural forms, creating lines of influence and solidarity different from, but no less meaningful than those observable within geographically circumscribed communities.[4]

These transformations require, of those studying popular music, more than well-intended gestures in the direction of multicultural diversity. They invite an attention to the distinctive logics of change and forms of valorization characteristic of different musical practices, as these are disseminated through their respective cultural communities and institutional sites. Two specific examples of this system of articulation – those characteristic of the cultures of alternative rock and dance music – will be discussed in detail later in this essay. In each case, and perhaps unsurprisingly, one may find distinctive relationships between localism as a musical value and the articulatory system of which Said speaks.

Canadian academics who are engaged in speaking and writing about popular music, like myself, sometimes express our growing scepticism at the way in which intermittent returns to older musical traditions by popular musicians within Canada and Quebec have been enshrined as moments of disengagement from the functioning of the international music industries. The Québécois folk-rock of the early 1970s and country-rock of English-Canadian post-punk cultures offer rich and valued examples of successful national traditions, and their place within historical accounts is well deserved. At the same time, however, each emerged within international industrial and cultural contexts which shaped the conditions of existence and certain of the 'meanings' of musical localism throughout Western countries. This interlocking of local tendencies and cyclical transformations within the international music industries is particularly striking in the case of contemporary Quebec, whose recording industry has been revitalized by an ongoing series of dance-pop stars passing from music-video networks to Top 40 radio and television talk shows.

At the same time, the criteria of public support for popular recordings within Canada frequently presume patterns of career development, forms of collaboration and a relationship between domestic and international popularity which implicitly privilege the rock group over the dance-music production team, the album over the single, and the gradual building of an audience base over the rapid circulation of recordings through a dispersed group of metropolitan centres. While at least five British music-oriented magazines have run recent cover stories on a Toronto rap group – The Dream Warriors – and the local contexts of its emergence, there is a striking absence of media coverage of this activity within Canada. One finds, at the same time, little sense that such activity corresponds to the objectives of domestic music-oriented policy or the concerns of those engaged in defining a national musical culture. Basing a politics of local or Canadian music on the search for musical forms whose relationship to musical communities is that of a long-term and evolving expressivity will lead us to overlook ways in which the making and remaking of alliances between communities are the crucial political processes within popular music.

The Carleton conference appeared to signal a relative decline in the importance of the United States as a privileged point of reference in discussions of popular music. There were obvious reasons for this: a reduction in the number of US-owned major recording firms, the much-diagnosed 'crisis' of rock music and its mythico-ideological bases, and the recent interest of popular-music scholars in public policies intended to achieve economic growth (a concern relatively rare within US research). Jody Berland's paper was, nevertheless, a useful reminder that the new globalization of the cultural industries is unlikely to alter regional or hemispheric patterns of economic subordination. Less certain, in the Canadian context, is the extent to which arguments for national economic self-determination in the music industries must necessarily be backed by claims of diminishing diversity or the isolation of national musical forms for protection. Amidst the observable busyness of metropolitan music scenes – and given the noticeable fragmentation of musical tastes among academics, their students, and music policy-makers – arguments in defence of domestic record manufacturing and distribution facilities posed in the language of economic viability have increasingly displaced debates over the sorts of music to be protected.

The heartland as collapsing centre

In November 1990, *Billboard* magazine published a front-page 'Special

Report' entitled 'Rock losing grip as other genres gain' (DiMartino and Duffy, 1990). The story which unfolded therein followed the familiar contours of accounts of centres which can no longer hold. What is declining, the report suggested, was mainstream rock of the so-called US 'heartland', of the sort associated with such artists as Tom Petty or John Cougar Mellencamp. More generally, it was claimed, the contemporary youth audience for popular music is being polarized between the 'extremes' of dance-based pop and heavy metal. As *Billboard*'s reporters made the rounds of record-company personnel seeking out reasons for this decline, a number of explanations were offered. This slump in mainstream rock was either cyclical, the result of popular music's political edge having moved, temporarily, into rap music; or it was a sign of the absence of new performers working this particular musical terrain. Some of those interviewed suggested simply sitting out what they called the era of 'fads' and disposable pop 'sound bites' until the durable values of Midwestern rock made their return.

The most revealing of these interviews was with Hugo Burnham, described as 'A & R director at Island Records and a punk survivor who once played drums with Gang of Four'. Burnham suggested that:

[R]ock music is losing ground because there's not an awful lot new that's happened to rock music since punk. . . . Since then, what is generally seen as rock music has been so regenerative stylistically and musically to the point where it's generic [*sic*]. The whole pop metal scene is all form over content. (DiMartino and Duffy, 1990: 100)

One need not share Burnham's judgement of these events to see within his diagnosis a recognition of important transformations within the culture of Western popular music. The decline of heartland rock as a specific form is less significant than is the more general waning of a distinctive sense (however fantasmatic) of rock music's centre – as involving the articulation of regional, authorial visions with a presumed affective appeal across the broad international culture of Western popular music. A view of rock music's history as an ongoing succession of such visions – questionable, in any case – is less and less appropriate when the 'regions' from which performers emerge are most often relatively insular (but geographically dispersed) generic traditions, or particular positions within the social relations of the Western city.

If, at one level, these changes are rooted in processes of internationalization and the diminished importance of the US market, then a comparison with the film industry suggests itself. Press coverage of that industry throughout 1990 and the early months of 1991 pointed repeatedly to a growing gulf between the domestic and international markets for US-made feature films. Most often, this gulf was described in terms of a difference between the small budgets deemed necessary to long-term industry health and the need, in order to achieve international success, for high production values and expensive stars. More elaborate readings of this situation offered versions of a no-more-*Driving-Miss-Daisies* scenario: the disappearance of unspectacular, dramatically complex and culturally specific low-budget films as a result of producers catering to the perceived needs of the international market (e.g., Turner, 1991; Landro, 1990).

This comparison is convincing if one accepts that the quasi-monopoly of the big-budget action film grows out of similar conditions to those which have brought about Hugo Burnham's triumph of form over content, and that the effects of these changes are identical. This is a correspondence, nevertheless, which I would wish to dispute. In the case of the film industry one does have, perhaps, evidence of the domination of what Michael Dorland has labelled films from 'the modern nowhere', texts partaking of a set of international generic shorthands (Dorland, 1987: 4).[5] If the condition of contemporary popular music is quite distinct, however, this is because processes of internationalization within it have served to reproduce a complex diversity – rather than a coherent uniformity – from one urban centre to another. While the consumption practices of film audiences are far from homogeneous, popular music is, nevertheless, marked to a much greater extent by its importance within processes of social differentiation and interaction. The drawing and enforcing of boundaries between musical forms, the marking of racial, class-based and gender differences, and the maintenance of lines of communication between dispersed cultural communities are all central to the elaboration of musical meaning and value. What the analyst may reconstruct in the case of the cinema – the correlation of tastes and consumption patterns with categories of social identity – is a much more explicit and resonant component of the sense music fans make of their own involvement in the culture of popular music.

In this respect, there is a certain clumsy aptness in Burnham's argument that rock has become 'generic', or that pop metal embodies the triumph of 'form over content'. In a very real sense, the social and cultural spaces within which dance-pop music or heavy metal flourish are likely to remain stable for the foreseeable future. Like virtually all those forms which have emerged in the last fifteen years, they are less likely to recede with cyclical change than continue to develop within the cultural spaces appropriate to them. The coherence of these spaces is rooted in such characteristics as their rates of change and turnover, the sorts of values attached, within them, to performer personae, and the forms and degrees of involvement in musical culture which they presume. While these characteristics may crystallize around particular musical forms, such as heavy metal, they are more usefully seen as defining musical terrains within which a variety of forms may be integrated.

Within this complex of cultural spaces, heartland rock will be seen as no more central and no less ethnically or racially specific than any other form. Its decline is due less to an internal ideological crisis of the rock project than to the ethnicization of white popular musical forms more generally. This ethnicization may be seen as the long-delayed recognition, in the case of forms often regarded as historically privileged or central, that their positioning (and that of their audiences) within a set of social and cultural relations is more determinant of their meanings than their genealogical heritage or capacity to evoke myths of community. Even within audiences which are predominantly white, the cultural terrain normally associated with mainstream, heartland rock has been fractured along the lines of age and taste: firstly, by the seemingly permanent institution of the alternative rock scene as the locus of musical activity for audiences involved in a connoisseurist fashion in rock music; secondly, by the continued importance of the young adolescent market to the turnover of successful records, and the alliance of this market with dance music and heavy metal; and, finally, by the hazy buying patterns of older adolescents and young adults, who are distributing their purchasing power across a wide array of catalogue or speciality materials newly available on compact disc.

TERMS OF ANALYSIS

In a suggestive paper, Barry Shanks has pointed to the usefulness of a notion of 'scene' in accounting for the relationship between different musical practices unfolding within a given geographical space (Shanks, 1988). As a point of departure, one may posit a musical scene as distinct, in significant ways, from older notions of a musical community. The latter presumes a population group whose composition is relatively stable – according to a wide range of sociological variables – and whose involvement in music takes the form of an ongoing exploration of one or more musical idioms said to be rooted within a geographically specific historical heritage. A musical scene, in contrast, is that cultural space in which a range of musical practices coexist, interacting with each other within a variety of processes of differentiation, and according to widely varying trajectories of change and cross-fertilization. The sense of purpose articulated within a musical community normally depends on an affective link between two terms: contemporary musical practices, on the one hand, and the musical heritage which is seen to render this contemporary activity appropriate to a given context, on the other. Within a musical scene, that same sense of purpose is articulated within those forms of communication through which the building of musical alliances and the drawing of musical boundaries take place. The manner in which musical practices within a scene tie themselves to processes of historical change occurring within a larger international musical culture will also be a significant basis of the way in which such forms are positioned within that scene at the local level.

At one level, this distinction simply concretizes two countervailing pressures within spaces of musical activity: one towards the stabilization of local historical continuities, and another which works to disrupt such continuities, to cosmopolitanize and relativize them. Clearly, the point is not that of designating particular cultural spaces as one or the other, but of examining the ways in which particular musical practices 'work' to produce a sense of community within the conditions of metropolitan music scenes. This move – recasting powerful unities as ideological effects – is obviously a familiar and rather conventional one within cultural theory, and my intention is not that of exposing the relative status of notions of musical community (in what my friend Don Wallace calls the now-it-can-be-told! rhetoric of anticlimatic revelation). Nevertheless, as subsequent sections of this essay will argue, the cosmopolitan character of certain kinds of musical activity – their attentiveness to change occurring elsewhere – may endow them with a unity of purpose and sense of participating in 'affective alliances' (Grossberg, 1984) just as powerful as those normally observed within practices which appear to be more organically grounded in local circumstances.

The ongoing debate within popular-music studies over the relative primacy of production and consumption has often precluded the analysis of what might be called the 'logics' of particular musical terrains.[6] I hope, in the sections which follow, to leave entangled three relevant prior uses of the term 'logic'. The first, drawn from Pierre Bourdieu's (e.g., 1979) notion of the 'field' of cultural practices, is meant to suggest those procedures through which principles of validation and means of accommodating change operate within particular cultural spaces so as to perpetuate their boundaries. It may be argued that the complex and contradictory quality of cultural texts – to which cultural studies research has been so attentive – has prevented neither their circulation within societies nor their alignment with particular population groups and cultural spaces from following regularized and relatively stable patterns. If this predictability is the result of semantic or ideological contradictions within these texts usually being resolved in favour of one set of meanings over others, then an analysis of these more general patterns, rather than of the conflicts which unfailingly produce them, may have a provisional usefulness at least.

The specificity of these 'fields', nevertheless, is shaped in part by the 'regions' they occupy, as markets and contexts of production, relative to a given set of cultural institutions. Bernard Miège's (1986: 94) elaboration of a 'social logic' of cultural commodities, while concerned principally with processes of production, may be extended to an examination of the ways in which cultural commodities circulate within their appropriate markets and cultural terrains. If there is a specificity to cultural commodities, it has much to do with the ways in which their circulation through the social world is organized as a lifecycle, in the course of which both the degree and basis of their appeal is likely to change.[7] Different cultural spaces are marked by the sorts of temporalities to be found within them – by the prominence of activities of canonization, or by the values accruing to novelty and currency, longevity and 'timelessness'. In this respect, the 'logic' of particular musical culture is a function of the way in which value is constructed within them relative to the passing of time. Similarly, cultural commodities may themselves pass through a number of distinct markets and populations in the course of their lifecycles. Throughout this passage, the markers of their distinctiveness and the bases of their value may undergo significant shifts.[8]

Finally, and in what is admittedly an act of trivialization and infidelity, I would take from the writings of Michel de Certeau (1990) the sense of a logic of circumstantial moves. The preoccupation of music sociologists with the expressive substance of musical forms has often obscured the extent to which particular instances of change might best be explained in terms of an as-yet elusive microsociology of backlashes or of failed and successful attempts at redirection within a given cultural terrain. This is particularly true in the case of contemporary dance-music culture, where, one might argue, there is little rationality to certain 'moves' (such as the 'Gregorian House' moment of early 1991) beyond the retrospective sense of appropriateness produced by their success. The risk of an analysis pursued along these lines is that it will result in little more than a formalism of cyclical change. One may nevertheless see the logic of these moves as grounded in the variable interaction between two social processes: (a) the struggles for prestige and status engaged in by professionals and others (such as disc jockeys) serving as 'intellectuals' within a given musical terrain; and (b) the ongoing transformation of social and cultural relations – and of alliances between particular musical communities – occurring within the context of the contemporary Western city. An attentiveness to the interaction between these two processes is necessary if one is to avoid either of two traps: on the one hand, privileging the processes within popular musical culture which most resemble those of an 'art world' and overstating the directive or transformative force of particular agents within them; on the other, reading each instance of musical change or synthesis as unproblematic evidence of a reordering of social relations.

Localizing the cosmopolitan: the culture of alternative rock

By the early or mid-1980s, a terrain of musical activity commonly described as 'alternative' was a feature of virtually all US and Canadian urban centres. In one version of its history, the space of alternative rock is seen to have resulted from the perpetuation of punk music within US and Canadian youth culture, a phenomena most evident in the relatively durable hardcore and skinhead cultures of Los Angeles and elsewhere. As local punk scenes stabilized, they developed the infrastructures (record labels, performance venues, lines of communication, etc.) within which a variety of other musical activities unfolded. These practices, most often involving the eclectic revival and transformation of older musical forms, collectively fell under the sign of the term 'alternative'. As the centrality of punk within local musical cultures declined, the unity of alternative rock no longer resided in the stylistic qualities of the music embraced within it. Rather, as I shall argue, that unity has come to be grounded more fundamentally in the way in which such spaces of musical activity have come to establish a distinctive relationship to historical time and geographical location.

Arguably, the most notable feature of alternative-rock culture over the last decade or so has been the absence within it of mechanisms through which particular musical practices come to be designated as obsolete. By the middle of the 1980s, the pluralism of alternative-rock culture was such that the emergence of new stylistic forms within it would rarely be accompanied by the claim that such forms represented a trajectory of movement for that culture as a whole. On the contrary, those processes by which musical forms become central poles of attraction and are subsequently rendered obsolete had largely disappeared. One may contrast this condition with that of the period immediately following the emergence of punk in Great Britain. There, one finds a preoccupation with finding pre-existent forms which might sustain the cultural space of punk, and a sense that these forms – whether revived, like the Mod sound of the 1960s, or borrowed laterally, from funk or reggae – might serve as poles of collective attraction for post-punk culture as a whole. This retrieval of earlier forms or appropriation of adjacent forms participated in a more general enterprise of finding the form appropriate to the next collective move in an ongoing transformation of rock-music culture and its values.

Within the US and Canada, the relationship between the different musical practices undertaken within the terrain of alternative rock would become one of lateral expansion. Within this terrain, different musical practices came to map out a range of increasingly specific stylistic combinations within an ongoing process of differentiation and complexification. Change within the culture of alternative rock, to the extent that it was observable at all, more and more took the form of new relationships between generic styles constitutive of the canon which had sedimented within alternative-rock culture since the late 1970s. It was no longer the case, as it had been in the period immediately following punk, that change would involve the regular displacement of styles as the historical resonance of each emerged and faded. The stabilization of this distinct temporality has had its most profound effects on the relationship between alternative culture and African-American musical forms, with the latter standing implicity for a relationship to technological innovation and stylistic change against which the former has come to define itself.

To understand this condition, we may examine the role still played within the terrain of alternative rock by musical cross-fertilization and hybridization. Here, the exercise of combining styles or genres will rarely produce the sense of a synthesis whose constituent elements are displaced, or through which musical communities are brought into new alliances, as has been the case at particular transitional points within rock history. Rather, one sees the emergence of a wide variety of stylistic or generic exercises, in which no style begins as privileged or as more organically expressive of a cultural point of departure. One effect of this has been to install the individual career, rather than the culture of alternative rock as a whole, as the principal context within which change is meaningful. Moves within this culture – from punk to country, psychedelia to boogie blues, and so on – represent idiosyncratic passages across the space of alternative rock rather than attempts at collective redirection.

This characteristic of the terrain of alternative rock has both shaped and responded to the commodity forms which circulate within it. In its reliance on the institutional infrastructures of campus radio stations, independent record stores, and live performance tours, alternative rock has been allied with institutions engaged in the valorization of their exhaustivity and diversity, and in maintaining the accessibility of a wide range of musical practices. The slowness of turnover which this produces is linked to the growth in importance of performer careers, inasmuch as the value of a particular recording is not dependent upon its capacity to register collective change within the larger cultural space in which it circulates. In this respect, the much-discussed 'co-optation' of punk and post-punk musics by major recording firms represents, in part, a paradoxical convergence of operational logics. Of the various forms of appropriation of these musics attempted by major firms, the most successful has been the ongoing monitoring of alternative-rock culture (often through the setting-up or affiliation of specialty labels) so as to discover careers susceptible to further development.

One effect of these processes has been an intermittently observed sense of crisis within the culture of alternative rock music. As suggested, the capacity of this culture to cater to the most specific of taste formations is accompanied by the sense that no particular stylistic exercise may be held up as emblematic of a collective, forward movement on the part of this terrain as a whole. Simon Reynolds has described the ways in which the self-valorization of alternative rock had come, by the early 1980s, to take the form of gestures towards the busyness and pluralistic health of small-scale musical activity rather than of claims to a collective and transgressive assault (however imaginary) on the dominant forms or institutions of popular musical culture.[9] The organization of alternative rock culture in these terms has had two significant – and generally overlooked – consequences which any political diagnosis of that culture must confront. These extend beyond the more general (and not necessarily negative) waning of collective purpose and criteria of judgement common within cultural spaces marked by high levels of pluralism and eclecticism.

The first of these is the enshrining of specific forms of connoisseurship as central to an involvement in alternative musical culture. Here, an alternative reading of the stabilization of post-punk culture within the US and Canada suggests itself. Despite the difficulty of reconstructing this historical context, I would point to the important interaction, in the mid and late 1970s, between the terrain of punk and 'New Wave' and pre-existing connoisseurist tendencies within the culture of rock music. To a considerable extent, the institutions of New Wave within the United States and Canada came to overlap with those constitutive of a network of enterprises catering to an interest in the history of rock-based forms of recorded music – an infrastructure which had existed at least since the early 1970s. These institutions were active in the historical documentation and revival of a variety of older rock-based musical movements (such as 'surf' music or the 'garage-band' movement of the mid-1960s.)[10] From the mid-1970s through to the present, a variety of small enterprises have involved themselves simultaneously in projects of historical revival (reissuing recordings from the 1960s and publishing fan magazines devoted to older musical forms) and in the production, distribution and sale of recordings associated with punk and those tendencies which succeeded it.[11]

This overlapping of alternative-rock culture and the cultural space of records collectors and historical archivism should scarcely be surprising, given the predictable settling of both within the sociological limits of a largely white bohemia. Part of the implicit work of alternative-rock culture over the past decade has been the construction of a relatively stable canon of earlier musical forms – 1960s trash psychedelia, early 1970s metal, the dissident rock tradition of the Velvet Underground and others – which serves as a collective reference point. The substance of this canon is less significant, at this point in my account, than is the fact that the cultivation of connoisseurship in rock culture – tracking down old albums, learning genealogical links between bands, and so on – has traditionally been one rite of passage through which the masculinism of rock-music culture has been perpetuated. Many of the temporary and transversal moves common in the early days of New Wave – moving from theatre or performance art into bands, or playing around with the forms of earlier, pre-rock musics – came to seem less and less appropriate or frequent as the 1980s wore on, and as the association of entry into alternative-rock culture with an activity of apprenticeship became entrenched. With these developments, the profile of women as performers within post-punk culture has diminished, and, just as the culture of alternative rock within the United States and Canada has become almost exclusively white, it has become overwhelmingly male as well.

A second consequence of the logic of development of alternative-music culture within Canada and the US is the paradoxical status of localism within it. In their reliance on small-scale infrastructures of production and dissemination, these spaces are rooted deeply within local circumstances, a feature commonly invoked in claims as to their political significance. Nevertheless, the degree to which localism remains an important component of musical meaning within the culture of alternative rock requires close examination. The aesthetic values which dominate local alternative terrains are for the most part those of a musical cosmopolitanism wherein the points of musical reference are likely to remain stable from one community to another. The development of alternative-rock culture may be said to follow a logic in which a particular pluralism of musical languages repeats itself from one community to another. Each local space has evolved, to varying degrees, the range of musical vernaculars emergent within others, and the global culture of alternative rock music is one in which localism has been reproduced, in relatively uniform ways, on a continental and international level.

One consequence of this condition is that the relationship of different local or regional scenes to each other is no longer one in which specific communities emerge to enact a forward movement to which others are drawn. What has declined is the sense, important at different moments within rock music's history, that a regional or local style offers the direction for change deemed appropriate to a given historical moment and provides a particular trajectory of progress which others will follow. Rather, the relationship of different local spaces of activity to each other takes the form of circuits, overlaid upon each other, through which particular styles of alternative music circulate in the form of recordings or live performances.

The ability of groups and records to circulate from one local scene to another, in a manner that requires little in the way of adaptation to local circumstances, is an index of the way in which a particularly stable set of musical languages and relationships between them has been reproduced within a variety of local circumstances.

Drawing lines, making centres: the culture of dance music

> Out on the dancefloor there are plenty more tell-tale signs to let you know if you're in the wrong sort of club. The music is always a giveaway, especially if the DJ still thinks it's a good idea to play 'French Kiss' or other similar rubbish. DJ's who prefer to show off their mixing skills rather than play good music are always worth avoiding, as are most of those who decide to adopt silly names (Crysell, 1990).

Several years ago, at the end of a conference held at Carleton University, I went with a number of academic colleagues to Hull, Quebec to dance. We ended up at the most explicitly 'underground' of the many clubs along Hull's main street (one whose recent history has been marred by door-admittance policies and changes in musical style widely regarded as racist). As members of our group began to dance – with, in some cases, unexpected abandon – it was clear that the space of this club, like the act of dancing itself, evoked within many of them a sense of the eternal. The club, its clientèle and the music being played all signified the transhistoricity of a youth culture which one might visit intermittently and find unchanged, and the act of dancing itself was intimately bound up with a generalized sense of diminished inhibition. It occurred to me that the principal differences between our group and the rest of those in attendance were not the expected ones of age and temperament. Rather, they seemed rooted in the unity academics were quick to ascribe to a cultural space which was characterized, more than most others, by the marking of distinction and drawing of boundaries.[12]

As list of the levels on which this marking is carried out would be virtually without end. Dance clubs are positioned relative to others, not only along the predictable lines of musical style, age, sexual orientation and ethnicity, but in terms of a variety of less frequently acknowledged criteria: the explicitness of sexual interaction within them, the manner in which their DJ handles the tension between playing requests and retaining prestige within his peer community, the level of tolerance of deviations from expected behavioural norms and so on. Among a club's clientèle, further distinctions take shape around the degree to which people dance within disciplined parameters (as opposed to cutting loose), or such minor clues as whether or not one remains on or leaves the dance floor when a new and as-yet unpopular song is played. Most importantly, the composition of audiences at dance clubs is likely to reflect and actualize a particular state of relations between various populations and social groups, as these coalesce around specific coalitions of musical style.

The significance invested in these differences obviously works against one familiar reading of the experience of dance: as a transcendent experience of the body in motion. The difficulty of writing about dance music is very much rooted in what Jane K. Cowan, speaking of a very different context, has called 'the paradoxically double sense of engrossment and reflexivity that characterize the experience of the dancer' (Cowan, 1990: xi). Discussions of dance are often able to privilege its engrossing qualities through an implicit sliding from the subjective and corporal sense of release to a notion of collective transcendence, such that the personal and the social are united under the sign of the term 'youth'. Clearly, however, few cultural practices are marked so strongly by the intervention of differences which fracture that unity and render unavoidable the reflexivity of which Cowan writes. Bringing together the activities of dance and musical consumption, the dance club articulates the sense of social identity as embodied to the conspicuous and differential display of taste. As such, it serves to render explicit the distribution of knowledges and forms of cultural capital across the vectors of gender, race and class.

It is at this point that we may begin to outline certain divergences between the cultures of alternative rock and dance music. The most significant of these, arguably, has to do with the manner in which each has responded to the hierarchies and tensions produced by the aforementioned differences. The ongoing development of dance-music culture is shaped by the relationship between certain relatively stable social spaces (whether these be geographical regions or racial and ethnic communities) and the temporal processes produced and observable within that culture's infrastructures (record labels, dance-music magazines, disc-jockey playlists, and so on). As suggested earlier, this relationship is not one of direct mirroring. The lines of fracture which run through the audiences of dance music are normally turned into the bases of that music's own ongoing development, but in this process they are often transformed. Typically, they are restated in the language of aesthetic choice and invoked as the pretexts for moves of redirection. In the culture of alternative rock, in contrast, the most consistent development has been the drawing of lines around that culture as a whole, such that certain forms (classically soulful voices, for example) are permanently banished, or, like some uses of electronics, tolerated as part of a circumscribed pluralism. (In neither instance do they serve as the basis of a tension inviting a collective response.)

These differences may be expressed in more schematic terms. The terrain of alternative rock is one in which a variety of different temporalities have come to coexist within a bounded cultural space. There is often a distinctive density of historical time within the performance styles of alternative groups: most noticeably, an inflection of older, residual styles with a contemporary irony which itself evokes a bohemian heritage in which that combination has its antecedents. Similarly, as moves within alternative rock produce more and more detailed syntheses of style and form, they fill in the range of options between canonical styles, the latter serving (to disinter a once-prominent theoretical concept) as 'points de capiton' (Lacan, 1966: 503), markers of privileged antecedents from which eclectic stylistic exercises develop outwards. This process as a whole might be described as one in which temporal movement is transformed into cartographic density.

The culture of dance music, in contrast, is one in which spatial diversity is perpetually reworked as temporal sequence. At one level, dance-music culture is highly polycentric, in that it is characterized by the simultaneous existence of large numbers of local or regional styles – Detroit 'techno' music, Miami 'bass' styles, Los Angeles 'swingbeat', etc. Other regional centres – like New York or London – will be significant, less as places of emergence of styles one could call indigenous, than because they occupy positions of centrality as sites for the reworking and transformation of styles originating elsewhere. Dance-music culture is characterized by two sorts of directionality: one which draws local musical activity into the production styles of one or more dominant, indigenous producers or sounds; and another which articulates these styles elsewhere, into centres and processes of change monitored closely by the international dance-music community as a whole. One effect of these sorts of movement is that coexisting regional and local styles within dance music are almost always at different stages within their cycles of rising and declining influence. A comfortable, stable international diversity may rarely be observed.[13]

Further evidence of these differences may be found in the sorts of publications which circulate within each terrain. *Maximum Rock and Roll* or *Rock Around The World: The Alternative Live Music Guide* manifest the preoccupation of alternative culture with cataloguing diversity, offering dozens of 'scene' reports or touring schedules in each issue. Those publications which serve the dance-music community, in contrast, are striking for their concern with registering movement, ranking records and judging styles in terms of their place within ascendant or downward trajectories of popularity.[14] This distinction is hardly surprising – given, on the one hand, the self-definition of alternative rock as the locus of a rock classicism, and, on the other, the observable overlap of dance-music culture with both the turbulent space of Top 40 radio and a more subcultural terrain resembling (and interacting with) the world of vestimentary fashion. More interesting, for my purposes, are the ways in which both cultures have responded to the musical diversity found in each, endowing that diversity with distinctive values and relationships to change.

The intermittent sense of crisis within the culture of North American alternative rock, to which I referred earlier, is arguably rooted in the loss of a teleology of historical purpose of the sort which has often organized accounts of rock music's history. In its place, we find enshrined a pluralism evoked as a sign of health and vitality. Within the culture of dance music, in contrast, a condition of pluralism is commonly cited as the sign of imminent troubles or divisions, rather than of that culture's richness or stability.[15] One finds, within the dance community, an investment in historical movement based almost exclusively on the ability of that movement to suggest collective purpose. Processes of historical change within dance music, as suggested, respond to shifting relationships between different (primarily urban) communities, but there is little sense that the convergences or alliances produced are permanent or constitutive steps in a movement towards a final dissolution of boundaries. Well-known moments held to be emblematic of a new unity of black and white youth cultures, like the punk-reggae moment of the late 1970s, either produce their own backlashes or appear in retrospect as temporary acts of rejuvenation undertaken by one of the communities involved.

The discursive labour of dance music's infrastructures operates implicitly to prevent the fractures and lines of difference which run through the culture of metropolitan dance music from either fragmenting that culture into autonomous, parallel traditions, or producing a final unity which will permanently paper over those lines. Like the worlds of fashion and painting, the dance music community accomplishes this by restating ongoing disagreements over cultural purpose and value as calculations about the imminent decay or emergent appropriateness of specific generic styles. One revealing example, within the recent history of dance music, is the ongoing controversy over the comparative appeal of synthesized sounds and 'real' human voices. The highly electronic acid house of 1987 and 1988 gave way, in influential corners of dance-music culture, to the 'garage' house of 1988–9, a form which valorized classic, soulful and identifiable voices. In 1990, and in the context of an increased rapidity of cyclical change, synthesized and sample-dominated Italian house emerged as central, accompanied by defences which underscored its knowing cleverness. Italian house was then displaced by the slowed-down, more obviously 'classical' Soul II Soul sound, which briefly, but spectacularly, attained international success. Predictably, a backlash followed, and Italian house was newly valorized at the beginning of 1991 – the 'tackiness' with which it had been marked during its brief banishment now regarded as a creative eclecticism.[16] These shifts, while obviously trivial and localized, nevertheless revolve at a fundamental level around the appropriate centrality to be accorded the traditions of African-American vocal music relative to those of a primarily white, European studio wizardry. Most often, however, they are given the form of oppositions of taste susceptible to regular revision: high- versus low-end sonic ranges, 'live' versus creatively manufactured sounds, the purist versus the novel, and so on.

At the same time, these oppositions represent implicit tensions over the appropriate status of creativity within dance-music culture: should that culture produce durable performer careers, most often those of (predominantly female) vocalists, or should its continuing development be driven by a turnover of rapidly obsolete (and almost exclusively male) record producers and small labels? Within the context of the multinational recording industry, of course, these tensions are resolved in ways that have little to do with the temporary prominence of certain values within the more insular culture of the dance community. Albums by the studio-based Italian house group Black Box and the white English soul singer Lisa Stanfield have each circulated in similar fashion within the international recording industry, producing a succession of singles and building their success through the sequence of dance clubs, Top 40 radio and music-video networks. If the implicit objects of investment in each case are different – a package of successive hits in the first case, a hopefully durable performer persona in the second – it is important to note that both presume different temporal logics than those currently typical of the dance community.

The circulation of records out of that community and cultural space relocates them in new contexts wherein the bases of their individual value and historical intelligibility are transformed.[17] The effort to realign these temporalities is evident in the recent move towards installing the compilation album (bringing together several extended dance cuts) as the principal medium through which major record companies will market dance music. With their coherence based on little more than the capacity to encapsulate a brief period in the ongoing history of dance music, compilation albums absolve major firms of the task of redefining the value of dance records in terms (most often those of performer careers or coherent works) which are familiar to them but incompatible with the forms of valorization common within the dance-music community.[18]

The condition of dance music described here – in particular, its rates and logics of change – has been intensified in recent years by the rise to prominence of house music. House music emerged (from Chicago) as a set of distinct styles in the mid-1980s, but its larger importance comes from its recentring of the historical movement of dance-music culture as a whole. As was the case prior to the rise of house, dance-music within the Western world has continued to be marked by opposed tendencies towards unity/coherence and diversity/differentiation, but the logics through which these processes unfold have become much more integrated. On the one hand, house music has drawn most dance-based musical forms into various sorts of accommodation to it. Currents within rap were compelled to adapt, most notably through an increased tempo, giving rise to forms known as hip-house and swingbeat. The Hi-NRG music associated during the previous decade with gay discos was revitalized as high-house, 'high' signalling a greater number of beats-per-minute than was the average within house music (Ferguson, 1991). Older or more eclectic forms, like industrial dance music and versions of jazz, have often been drawn into a sequence of transformations within house music, as influences defining those transformations. Those dance forms which did not lend themselves to this integration, for a variety of reasons – Go-Go music from Washington, or the Minneapolis sound associated with Prince and his collaborators – have been marked with relative obsolescence, at least as far as international success is concerned.

At the same time, however, the durability and expansiveness of appeal of house music are such that these variations have come to be positioned laterally within a division of tastes running across dance-music culture. The techno-pop and Hi-NRG associated with producers like Stock-Aitken-Waterman would, by the late 1980s, come to be positioned at one point within a continuum running through all forms of house music and overlapping with the terrain of international Top 40 pop. Much of Latin-based, English-language pop within the United States is now part of a complex of forms known as 'freestyle', in which one finds articulated elements of rap, house, and mainstream pop. More telling examples are those involving forms of dance music perpetuated within the space of a rock-based avant-garde. So-called New Beat music, associated principally with record labels based in Belgium, pulled elements of industrial dance rock into the overall culture of dance music, but simultaneously compelled industrial dance music to define itself in part through the vigilant maintenance of narrow boundaries between its own perceived transgressiveness and the lure of accessible, popular forms of house. One can see here the dilemma confronting tendencies within a post-punk avant-garde whose terrain has long bordered that of dance music. On the one hand, their project has derived much of its credibility from the consistent and avowedly purist exploration of a limited set of stylistic and formal figures overlapping those found within currents of alternative rock (stark instrumentation, the use of 'found' voices from television, etc.). On the other hand, the culture of British dance music has so successfully redefined the terms of credibility as accruing from participation in an unfolding sequence of musical styles that their resistance to this history risks casting them as irrelevant.[19]

My emphasis, here, on the logics of change typical of different musical terrains is not intended to suggest that the value of such terrains is a function of their collective historical purpose. What these logics invite, however, is a reading of the politics of popular music that locates the crucial site of these politics neither in the transgressive or oppositional quality of musical practices and their consumption, nor uniformly within the modes of operation of the international music industries. The important processes, I would argue, are those through which particular social differences (most notably those of gender and race) are articulated within the building of audiences around particular coalitions of musical form. These processes are not inevitably positive or disruptive of existing social divisions, nor are they shaped to any significant extent by solitary, wilful acts of realignment. (Attempts to transform them into the bases of artistic strategy have generally failed, one notable recent exception being that of the group Living Colour). Typically, the character of particular audiences is determined by the interlocking operation of the various institutions and sites within which musics are disseminated: the schoolyard, the urban dance club, the radio format. These sites, themselves shaped by their place within the contemporary metropolis and aligned with populations along the lines of class and taste, provide the conditions of possibility of alliances between musical styles and affective links between dispersed geographical places.

There are any number of examples of this in the recent history of Canadian, US and Western European popular music: the coalescing of the original audience for disco around Hispanic, black and gay communities in the mid-1970s, or the unexpected alignment of country music and its traditional audiences with urban-based, adult-oriented radio stations in the early 1980s. The particular condition of alternative rock music culture, which I have described at length, has been shaped in part by the way in which coalitions of black teenagers, young girls listening to Top 40 radio, and urban club-goers have coalesced around a dance-music mainstream and its margins and thus heightened the insularity of white, bohemian musical culture. What interests me, as someone who studies musical institutions, is the way in which these alliances are produced, in part, through the overlapping logics of development of different forms. One reason why coalitions of musical taste which run from British dance culture through black communities in Toronto and significant portions of the young female market are possible is that these constituencies are all ones which value the redirective and the novel over the stable and canonical, or international circuits of influence over the mining of a locally stable heritage. The substance of these values is less important than are the alliances produced by their circulation within musical culture. One need neither embrace the creation of such alliances as a force for social harmony or condemn them as politically distracting to recognize their primacy in the ongoing politics of popular musical culture.

Notes

1 This section of my article includes remarks written especially for this issue of *Cultural Studies* and intended to supplement John Shepherd's introduction. Subsequent sections are made up of a substantially revised version of my own presentation at the conference.
2 This panel, which opened the conference and was repeated at Concordia University in Montreal the following week, was not based on written presentations and is not reproduced in this issue.
3 The work of Jody Berland represents, perhaps, the most sustained attempt to date to investigate the status of locality in popular music. See, for example, Berland (1990).
4 See, for a lengthy discussion of the conditions of an Atlantic African cultural diaspora, Gilroy (1987).
5 It should be noted that Dorland uses this phrase to describe a Québécois 'art' film, and that the sense of placelessness described is one typical of the elliptical, wilfully transgressive and auteurist neo-*film noir* produced in any number of countries in the late 1980s. I have adapted Dorland's phrase to describe the popular, blockbuster films said by press accounts to result from Hollywood's new reliance on the international market.
6 Having sacrificed the terms 'community' and 'scene' to other conceptual unities, 'terrain' is one of the few remaining options for designating the spaces I want to discuss. 'Field', with which it is virtually synonymous, suggests more of an exclusive reliance on the work of Pierre Bourdieu than I wish to convey.
7 This is, of course, partially a function of the extent to which cultural commodities participate in the processes of 'fashion', processes described with great insight in Wark (1991).
8 Disco records of the late 1970s, for example, circulated within: (a) connoisseurist sub-cultures attentive to minor moves within the ongoing history of disco music as generic form; (b) 'urban' radio station playlists wherein differences between records were effaced within the creation of a consistent sound signifying currency and sophistication; and (c) Top 40 radio programming which, by the end of the decade, had produced a sense of disco as a musical form deployed by a succession of distinct celebrity personalities.

9 'Fanzines: the lost moment', *Monitor* (no date or page numbers).
10 So-called 'garage' psychedelia was a transitional form between the music of small rock quartets of the early 1960s and the more elaborate psychedelic or 'acid' rock of the late 1960s. In 1972, Elektra Records released *Nuggets*, an influential retrospective anthology of this music.
11 The most important of these, arguably, were Bomp Records and Rhino Records, both based in California. Bomp Records was associated with a record store, a fan magazine (*Who Put The Bomp?*) devoted to rock music of the 1960s, a mail-order record sales service, and a record label which specialized in recordings by contemporary groups performing older musical styles. Rhino Records, similarly, began as a retail store and expanded to include a record company specializing in both contemporary, New Wave-oriented recordings and reissues of repertory from the 1960s. My discussion of these enterprises, and of this tendency within New Wave in a more general sense, is based on my sporadic reading, throughout the 1970s, of magazines published within this subculture, most notably *Who Put The Bomb?* See, as well, for detailed reports on this phenomena, the following: 'Punk rock store pulls big in L.A.', *Billboard*, 30 April 1977: 6; 'New Wave label: Bomp Records adds LP line', *Billboard*, 11 August 1979: 74; 'Despite hard times: indie rock labels survive', *Billboard*, 15 January 1983: 1; 'Capitol distribution pact opens new fields for Rhino', *Billboard*, 2 November 1985: 82.
12 I should add that my own posture here – as detached cataloguer of minute differences – is obviously no more appealing or less stereotypically academic than the one I am ascribing to others.
13 The example, already cited, of electronic 'techno' music from Detroit is a useful one here. Techno has developed over several years now, but its articulation within the international culture of dance music has been intermittent and often dependent on an alliance with other, more obviously novel and emergent forms (such as the electronic 'bleep' or ambient music of the last year) (see Cheeseman, 1991).
14 Examples of these magazines include the Canadian *Streetsounds*, the British *Jocks* and the American *Dance Music Report*. The analysis presented in this section is based on my regular reading of these and several other magazines, conversations with dance-record store staff and the buying of several hundred dance records over the last decade.
15 Throughout the latter part of 1990 and early months of 1991, the observable pluralism and fragmentation of dance-music culture was cited as proof that a collapse of the economic bases of dance music was coming. See, for example, Cheeseman (1991), Jones (1991a), Russell (1991).
16 See, for one account of this re-emergence, Jones (1991b). The rapidity of these cycles of change has much to do with the international dance community having turned towards British dance culture as the primary site in which moves of redirection are enacted. This turn itself represents the convergence of a number of events: the decline in vinyl production in the US and Canada, and consequent reliance of the dance community on imported 12-inch singles; the related integration of much African-American music (most notably rap) within the market for albums and resulting decline of the single within certain genres; the smallness and relative insularity of British musical culture, which has obviously quickened the pace of change; and the growing tendency for British club disc jockeys (many of them now stars in their own right) to tour the Western world, in the process picking up local records – from Italy, New York,

Germany, etc. – which are drawn into the turnover of dance music within Britain itself.
17 This has produced much-commented-upon difficulties in the trans-Atlantic passage of certain recent dance records: Candy Flip's 'Strawberry Fields Forever' was a success as an import within US and Canadian dance clubs months before being released domestically in those countries. DJs here, for whom that record's Soul II Soul-ish rhythms (and the more general enterprise of covering older songs within those rhythms) had ceased to hold much interest, were unwilling to give it the level of renewed club play needed to cross it over to Top 40 radio. See, for one account, the 'Dance Trax' column in *Billboard*, 27 October 1990: 33.
18 See, for discussions of the rise of compilation albums, Jones (1991a) and Flick (1991).
19 At the moment, industrial dance music functions as both the continuing refuge for 'masculinist' tendencies within dance culture resisting those forms designated as frivolous and co-opted, and as a style newly embraced by politicized segments of the gay community for whom it serves as a sign of the new militancy produced by the AIDS crisis. See, for one account of the turn away from Hi-NRG within gay dance culture, the article 'Queer bashes' (no author) in *The Face*, February 1991: 79.

Acknowledgements

Different versions of portions of this paper were presented at the Canadian Communications Association conference in Quebec City in 1989, the International Communications Association conference in Dublin in 1990 and at the Trent Institute for Studies in Popular Culture, Trent University (Peterborough, Ontario) in 1991. I would like to thank Morgan Holmes, Trevor Holmes and Alan O'Connor, among others, for their helpful comments and questions concerning certain of the ideas presented here.

References

Berland, Jody (1990) 'Radio space and industrial time: music formats, local narratives and technological mediation', *Popular Music*, 9: 179–92.
Bourdieu, Pierre (1979) *La Distinction: Critique sociale du jugement*. Paris: Les Editions de Minuit.
de Certeau, Michel (1990) *L'invention du quotidien. 1. arts de faire*. Paris: Gallimard (Folio). (Originally published 1980.)
Cheeseman, Phil (1991) 'Year review', *Jocks*, 52, February 1991: 16.
Cowan, Jane K. (1990) *Dance and the Body Politic in Northern Greece*. Princeton, New Jersey: Princeton University Press.
Crysell, Andy (1990) 'The wrong sort of club', *Rave!*, 16, June 17–July 1 1990: 38.
DiMartino, Dave and Duffy, Thom (1990) 'Rock losing grip as other genres gain', *Billboard*, 10 November 1990: 1, 100.
Dorland, Michael (1987) Review of *Un Zoo, la nuit*, *Cinema Canada*, September 1987: 37.
Ferguson, Dean (1991) 'HiNRG/Eurobeat', *Dance Music Report*, 24: 38.
Flick, Larry (1991) 'Dance acts get new exposure via compilations', *Billboard*, 16 March 1991: 1, 83.

Gilroy, Paul (1987) *There Ain't No Black in the Union Jack*. London: Hutchinson.

Grossberg, Larry (1984) 'Another boring day in paradise: rock and roll and the empowerment of everyday life', *Popular Music*, 4: 225–58.

Jones, Alan (1991a) 'Dance file', *Jocks*, 51: 40.

—— (1991b) 'Dance file', *Jocks*, 53: 36.

Lacan, Jacques (1966) *Ecrits*. Paris: Editions du Seuil.

Landro, Laura (1990) 'Warner Bros. success at box office feeds its global ambitions', *The Wall Street Journal*, 1 June 1990: 1.

Miège, Bernard (1986) 'Les logiques à l'oeuvre dans les nouvelles industries culturelles', *Cahiers de recherche sociologique*, 4 (2) 93–110.

Russell, Deborah (1991) 'Grass route', *Billboard*, 5 January 1991: 56.

Said, Edward (1990) 'Figures, configurations, transfigurations', *Race & Class*, 32 (1), 1–16.

Shanks, Barry (1988) 'Transgressing the boundaries of a rock 'n' roll community'. Paper delivered at the 'First Joint Conference of IASPM-Canada and IASPM-USA', Yale University, 1 October 1988. [IASPM is the International Association for the Study of Popular Music.]

Turner, Richard (1991) 'Disney seeks to end big, big pictures as executive calls for small, small world', *The Wall Street Journal*, 30 January 1991: B1.

Wark, McKenzie (1991) 'Fashioning the future: fashion, clothing, and the manufacturing of post-Fordist culture', *Cultural Studies*, 5 (1) 61–76.

Will Straw is Assistant Professor and Program Co-ordinator of Film Studies within the School for Studies in Art and Culture at Carleton University, Ottawa

▪ REVIEWS ▪

PATRICE FLECK
PORNOTOPIA?

■ Linda Williams, *Hard Core. Power, Pleasure, and the 'Frenzy of the Visible'* (London: Unwin Hyman, 1990) £20.00.

Linda Williams's book provides a valuable contribution to the debate about pornography from an 'anti-censorship' feminist point of view; her work is in tension with anti-pornography/pro-censorship feminists such as Andrea Dworkin, Bonnie Klein, and Robin Morgan. Inflected by theories of psychoanalysis, Marxism and Foucault, *Hard Core* attempts to situate and historicize heterosexual cinematic and video hard-core pornography from the early illegal 'stag' films to the recent 'Femme' productions made by women pornographers. Williams uses a feminist-revisionist approach, focusing on issues of spectatorship that suggest that advent of a gradually evolving female subjectivity in narrative hard core. Believing that feminist critics must get beyond their 'gut responses' to pornography which enable them only to ask the tired question of whether or not hard core is misogynistic, Williams points out that porn is an intersection of knowledge and power operating on the bodies of women. She believes feminists must raise questions about porn's popularity and examine how these 'pleasures of the body' are subject to change in conjunction with historical and social constructions of female and male sexuality (p. 3).

Importantly, Williams locates the main problem of censorship feminists in their assumption that there exists 'a whole and natural sexuality that stands outside of history and free of power' (p. 23). An anti-censorship position, on the other hand, is against the notion of any '"politically correct", ideal sexuality' and defends the right to represent diverse sexualities (p. 23).

Williams begins her discussion of the history of cinematic hard core by locating its origins as a trajectory of what Foucault calls 'scientia sexualis' in

The History of Sexuality (1978), defined as the impulse that 'constructs modern sexualities according to a conjunction of power and knowledge' while investigating 'confessable "truths" of a sexuality that governs bodies and their pleasures' (p. 34). This will to pornographic visual knowledge occurs, Williams argues, with the invention of cinema, spawned by the desire to see bodily movement reproduced as Muybridge's photographic experiments suggest. It is this scopic drive for 'maximum visibility' of bodily movement that animates pornography's desire to see the 'truths' of orgasmic confession of the female body. Williams says that 'the woman's ability to fake the orgasm that the man can never fake . . . seems to be at the root of all the genre's attempts to solicit what it can never be sure of: the out of control confession of pleasure' (p. 50). One should note, however, the claim that this dynamic exists at the 'root' of all the genre's investigation: as a heterosexually oriented explanation, the theory implies that heterosexual male desires initiate all hard core, which does not account for lesbian and gay porn emanating from different sexualities and different scopic drives. An instance of the embeddedness of this heterosexual bias in the book is also evident in her discussion of the 'money shot', the industry's term for the isolated close-up of penile ejaculation most prevalent in narrative porn of the 1970s. Describing it as a Marxian and Freudian fetish, Williams calls the money shot 'a poor substitute for knowledge of female wonders that the genre as a whole still seeks' (p. 94), a statement that disallows the possibility of pleasure through alternative sexual orientation that would not necessarily be centred on a phallic/lack paradigm. I appreciate Williams's explanation for choosing to focus exclusively on heterosexual pornography because it is that which she believes most clearly addresses her; however, I think the issues she raises cannot be viewed in isolation from gay and lesbian pornography or spectatorship.

The greatest strengths of *Hard Core* lie in its documentation of pornography's generic evolution and its discussion of the changing possibilities of the female spectator throughout porn's history. Beginning with the illegal 'primitive stag', (*circa* 1907–60), the first codified type of hard core, Williams notes its exclusive appeal to male identification. Many of these films begin as narratives from a male character's voyeuristic point of view (looking through keyholes, etc.) and escalate to a succession of nonnarrative 'meat shots', which are close-ups of penetration and other hard-core activity, mostly female genitalia in this case. The pure spectacle of these shots is unconnected with any spectator position, but Williams claims that the male spectator has already been sutured in place, leaving no possibility for the female to gain pleasure.

The next significant development in hard-core pornography occurs during the 1970s when the genre became much more mainstream. No longer illegal, its primary form is now the narrative feature film (of which *Deep Throat* and *Behind the Green Door* are the most famous examples) which played in many first-run theatres, now attracting a female as well as a male audience. In an iconographic study of these films' various sexual 'numbers', Williams likens 1970s narrative porn to the Hollywood musical, replete with certain 'conventional' sexual numbers, and, as Rick Altman notes in *The American Film Musical*, with two centers of power: the male and the female. Williams notes pornographer Stephen Ziplow in his *Film Maker's Guide to Pornography* (1977), for whom certain 'required' numbers of the genre include masturbation, straight male-female penetration, lesbianism, oral sex, cunnilingus and fellatio, *ménage-à-trois*, orgies (but 'expensive') and anal sex if the receiver is female. Williams suggest that with these developments, porn is no longer focused exclusively on the heterosexual couple or on the primarily passive female as in the stag, but has become open to accommodate a multiplication of knowledge about different sex acts as well as the possibility of male and female spectatorial identification and pleasure.

Further refining the metaphor of the musical, Williams demarcates three specific types of film 'utopias' corresponding to different types of musicals. She identifies the 'separated utopia' first, as the most misogynistic and phallocentric. It corresponds to musicals in which the numbers are separated from the narrative as in Busby Berkeley's work, providing pure spectatorial pleasure of the female body. In hard-core equivalents, the woman's story is not part of the narrative but severed from it, making her into a quiescent spectacle. The 'integrated utopia', on the other hand, corresponds to musicals that incorporate numbers into the narrative as do many Astaire/Rogers films. This style provides a forum for the issues of the female characters of hard core. For example, even if a rape is depicted but is considered 'bad' from the woman's perspective, it no longer exists as spectacle alone, but raises questions of rape extending beyond a sole consideration of male pleasure. A final subgenre of the pornotopias is the 'dissolved utopia' which evaporates the distinction between fantasy and narrative reality; these films document a sexual dreamworld and are often *about* pleasing a female subject. Williams takes pains to describe these different subgenres thoroughly as she documents that hard core is no longer driven solely by a phallic standard of measurement.

Interspersed between these seventies utopian films and her discussion of pornography made by women, is a chapter on the sado-masochistic subgenre. Williams attempts to detoxify the 'concentration camp pornography' image of S/M perpetuated by Andrea Dworkin and other anti-porn feminists by drawing attention to the complexity of the contractual nature of the S/M relationship and the identificatory positions of female spectators. Even though the woman is usually the submissive one of an S/M pair, Williams argues that she is engaging in activities in search of her own pleasure. A potential for a bi-sexual 'oscillating' identification can occur but, interestingly, Williams asserts that identification with a totally powerless victim will not take place. This notion raises moral questions for this reviewer about the recuperation of S/M hard core for feminism and the responsibility of the critic; if women can never 'identify' with a brutalized female victim, what political significance does their identification with the male sadist have? Also, this discussion doesn't address the issue of pleasure in female masochism as being a problem, as being a culturally specific problem of gender inscription that needs interrogation.

Williams revises previous notions of the 'snuff' film's status as hard-core pornography, claiming that generically it resembles the horror/slasher film more. According to studies she cites (Donnerstein, *The Questions of Pornography: Research Findings and Policy Implications*, 1987), slasher/horror films are apparently more provocative of male violence against women than is hard core. This is interesting and unexpected information, but I think that the cross-influence of the two genres is also important and should be addressed, but this task is beyond the scope of her book. Another issue that I find problematic is her willingness to table the issue of 'snuff' films after the film entitled *Snuff* was discovered to be the 'hoax' of a husband and wife film-making team known for their low-budget horror films with 'bizarre deaths' (p. 193). It is as if now that this one film has been reassuringly demystified, Williams feels the issue can be dropped instead of encouraging further investigation of the reputedly prolific genre.

Regarding hard core of the 1980s, Williams demonstrates the 'democratization' of the genre fueled by an increase in the video trade. She argues that the new availability of porn in the home has enabled many women greater access to hard core which is changing to meet their different desires. Importantly, the advent of female heterosexual pornographers (Femme productions) has resulted in a serious effort to visualize women's desire. These films are characterized by few if any money shots and they emphasize couples' sexuality; the mood of these narratives is distinctly more romantic and focuses on a 'dissolved utopian' world of women's fantasies.

In the final pages of *Hard Core*, Williams's tone may become a bit quixotic when she claims that a 'female pornotopia' could be at hand when hard core begins to scrutinize male pleasure as it has scrutinized female pleasure. Within this stance lies the assumption that this 'female pornotopia' is a heterosexual one while it also runs the risk of glossing over some really misogynist hard core being produced today. None the less, *Hard Core* is a valuable addition to a dialogue that has been dominated too long by a reductive, censorial perspective. It provides a useful contribution to issues of female spectatorship in a popular genre long neglected by scholars.

Patrice Fleck teaches and researches at the University of Pittsburgh

JOHN FROW

FACE VALUE?

■ Jane Gaines, *Likeness and the Law: Image Properties in the Industrial Age* (University of North Carolina Press: Chapel Hill, 1991)

In 1984 Jacqueline Kennedy Onassis sues Dior for violation of privacy. Dior have used an image of her in an advertisement portraying the mock wedding of a fictional couple, 'the Diors': her face can clearly be seen among the wedding guests, many of them celebrities. The legal and philosophical issues involved in the case seem to be these: does Onassis own the *image* of her face in the same way that she legally 'owns' her own face and her own person? Can she restrain others from using this image on the basis of a property right? Is there an abuse here of her right to the commercial exploitation of her own face and person? Or are her face and her person so widely familiar, so given over to history that they should be considered to be in the public domain?

Already we are caught up in the philosophical core of questions about the nature of personhood and its historical relation to the bourgeois category of private property; about the sedimentation of this category in the legal system; and about the ambiguous ontology of representations. But there is a further complication to this case: the face in the picture 'belongs' not to Onassis but to a lookalike, one Barbara Reynolds, a Washington secretary. Or does it?

In order to resolve the dilemmas posed by the case, the courts resort to a semiotic analysis which is at once sophisticated and crude. Recognizing the limitations of a referential analysis which would relate the face immediately and exclusively to the identity of its owner, they seek to identify that multiple semiosis by which the empirical real of the body of the lookalike works in its turn as a signifier of the concept 'Onassis'. Like Eco, they read the iconic sign not as immediate resemblance but as code. Personhood is constructed as a legal, not a 'natural' reality. At the same time, the courts move to establish a property right in the image, and to limit its semiotic plurality, by invoking the distinction between original and copy: Dior and Reynolds have infringed by 'passing off' a simulacrum in such a way as to cause confusion with the real thing. 'Passing off' is a term that belongs to trademark law, and the implication is that the basis for the protection of the image of Onassis is its value as commercial property – not the more traditional basis for privacy, injury to the person.

The account of this case explores one dimension of that legal metaphysics involving the relationship between the person, property, and the image which was opened up by Edelman in *Ownership of the Image*.[1] Edelman's book was terse and indicative, largely restricted to French law, and jurisprudential in its focus; Gaines's moves these questions into the centre of the concerns of cultural studies by situating them in relation to film theory and by moving into the rich area of US intellectual property law, the doctrinal complexity of which has to do with the complexity of the commercial relations of the movie industry, and more generally of the American culture industry. (Instead, the whole system of industrial production is ultimately based in processes of copying, and the replication of information is merely a small-scale model of it.) Her answers are illuminating both about the philosophical structure of legal doctrine, and about the system of industrial production of the image.

The first of the areas of intellectual property doctrine that Gaines analyzes through particular case studies involves the question of the ownership of the photographic image. One of the key cases concerns a portrait of Oscar Wilde by the New York photographer Napoleon Sarony. Photography – as Edelman had already demonstrated for French law – had been hampered for much of the nineteenth century by its status as a 'mechanical' mode of reproduction of the real, and had thus had difficulty establishing a concept of authorship which would restrict the free availability of photographic images. The problem is overcome late in the century by investing an act of will in the work: photography is said to involve creative choices about framing, about the disposition of the diegetic material, in short to embody elements of personal style akin to those which constitute the originality of a painting. As in all post-Romantic legal systems, the aesthetic concept of originality guarantees a property right which is derived from the uniqueness of the person but which then becomes transferable on the market. In fact the substantive concept of aesthetic originality tends to decay in American law into a more neutral, nonevaluative sense which simply indicates a point of departure and the fact of a work's not having been copied from another work. This shift, Gaines argues, reflects a general movement in intellectual property law away from a humanistic conception of the subject and towards the protection in the first instance of commercial rights.

If the personality of the photographer establishes a right in the work, however, what is the status of the other personality that informs it, that of the photographed subject? In terms of legal first principles, both have rights of personhood which establish a claim to ownership of the image; and the claim of the photographed subject is enhanced by photography's specific reality-effect, which seems to guarantee a connection and a continuity, both in law and in common sense, between image and personal identity. This forms the starting point for Gaines's discussion of Onassis's claim to ownership of the image of 'her' face. It is also crucial to the contest – one which involves large financial stakes – between movie companies and movie stars over the ownership of the star image.

Contracts of employment between production companies and stars tend to contain very detailed specifications of those conditions of service which relate to the manufacture and control of the star image: not just prescriptions concerning costume and make-up but constraints on roles, on the forms of acceptable publicity, on billing, and in general on the ways in which the star is prepared to be type-cast. A reading of these texts – which Gaines integrates nicely with an account of changing labour relations within the movie industry – makes clear the extent to which stardom is a commercial property, a manufactured product dependent on but separate from the person of the actor.

After World War II, actors increasingly constitute themselves as independent businesses for the marketing of their images, and increasingly enter into competition with the studios (especially in the area of product endorsement). The commercial logic of seeing stardom as a commodity, however, is that it should become a moveable asset independent of the living body of the actor. Enter, with appropriate poetic irony, the heirs of Bela Lugosi to claim a surviving right in the deathless piece of tangible property, the image of Dracula.

Their claim is staked on the basis of Lugosi's right to privacy: even after his death, they argue, his image should not be exploited in merchandising campaigns (and if his image *is* to be exploited, then his heirs should benefit from this continuing use of a property of which Lugosi was the rightful owner). The claim fails because the right to privacy is held to be rooted in the person and hence not to be assignable; but in the process a new right, the right to publicity, is invented by the courts, and is reinforced by Section 990 of the California Civil Code which grants a personal monopoly in the image and extends it for fifty years to the heirs of its deceased proprietor. In particular, it protects the image from various kinds of politically charged popular uses – send-ups and caricatures, for example. (The counter-example here is the judgement by a court in Tennessee – soon overturned by the state legislature – which had to decide the ownership of the 'fame' of Elvis Presley. It held that, since Presley's fame was constructed by the public, his image, and the associated souvenir and memorabilia industry, should properly belong in the public domain.)

The image has proved to be eminently protectable; sound has been less so, for reasons that Gaines explores in interesting depth. In a 1970 case Nancy Sinatra claimed to have established a 'secondary meaning' in her performance of a song as well as in her stylistic arrangement of it. Secondary meaning is a term of art designating the process by which words, names, designs, bodies – in short, signifiers – acquire an additional, special, and singular meaning which associates them with a commercial entity (camel, shell, tide, apple . . .). It is, you might say, the commodified state of signification. Trademark law has the double function of ensuring the free circulation of ordinary (or 'descriptive') meanings, and restricting the free circulation of these 'distinctive' meanings. Like all intellectual property law, it creates property rights in an immaterial commodity, information. In the case of phonic signifiers, however, for reasons which have to do with the relative undifferentiation of sound, the courts have been reluctant to extend protection. Similarly, 'style' and performance, as structures distinct from the work, have been found insubstantial to constitute protectable property. At the same time, however, Gaines sees the historical *development* of a proprietary right in the voice, parallel to the development of technologies of sound reproduction (which have made the voice more akin to a 'writing'); and a 1988 case pitting Bette Midler against the Ford Motor Company introduced the new criterion of a proprietary right in personal identity, and then (in a linkage which has become familiar) deduced from it a property value in the voice.

The final area covered in the book is that of trademark protection, which has traditionally been an alternative to, and even at times in contradiction with, copyright and privacy law. Originally intended as a guarantee to the public of the authenticity of a product, trademark has come above all to protect sellers from infringing competition, and to stand for market expansion and control. The paradigm case that Gaines examines here is that of the SUPERMAN trademark, which has been ruthlessly enforced by D. C. Comics in order to stamp out not only rival characters but also parodies and even the name of a school newspaper, the *Daley Planet*. Unlike copyright law, which allows 'fair uses' of original work, trademark makes possible a much more absolute private ownership of signifiers, and a corresponding reduction of the public domain.

Paradoxically, however, the very success of a trademark may result in its demise. Safari, aspirin, thermos, cellophane, formica: all have become household words and have accordingly lost their trademark protection – a fate which must surely be imminent for Superman. It is this absorption of protected material by the public domain, the appropriations and the rearticulations by which restricted meanings are given popular currency and are put to unpredictable or unwelcome uses, that forms the basis of the book's concluding political discussion, and indeed that gives it its continuous political edge.

Part of what's fascinating about the law's dealings with questions of aesthetics and signification is its insistent demand for clear enforceable answers to complex semiotic questions. Its usual practice is to make up the answers for itself, on the basis of legal first principles and doctrinal precedent. This means in effect that it draws upon an ideological common sense which is often the sedimentation of highly developed philosophical categories (the concepts of substance and expression or of original and copy in copyright law are examples). The combination of its naivety and its immense practical force makes it a strong provocation to theory – and something of this provocation shows in Gaines's extended theorization of historical changes in the author function, or of the ontology of sound, or of the relation between trademark and serial narrative structures. Both in these terms, and in terms of its sophisticated analysis of the juridical underpinnings of cultural production, the book makes a major contribution to cultural studies.

Notes

1 Bernard Edelman, *Ownership of the Image: Elements for a Marxist Theory of Law*, Trans. Elizabeth Kingdom. London: Routledge & Kegan Paul, 1979).

John Frow is Professor in the Department of English,
University of Queensland, Australia

INDEX
VOLUME 5

Articles

Tony Bennett	The shaping of things to come: Expo '88	p. 30
Jody Berland	Free trade and Canadian music: level playing field or scorched earth	p. 317
Marcus Breen	A stairway to heaven or a highway to hell?: heavy metal rock music in the 1990s	p. 191
Laurie Brown	Songs from the bush garden	p. 347
David Buckingham	What are words worth?: interpreting children's talk about television	p. 228
Sara Cohen	Popular music and urban regeneration: the music industries of Merseyside	p. 332
Maria Damon	Talking Yiddish at the boundaries	p. 14
Simon Frith	Anglo-America and its discontents	p. 263
John Frow	Michel de Certeau and the practice of representation	p. 52
Reebee Garofalo	The internationalization of the US music industry and its impact on Canada	p. 326
Andrew Goodwin	Popular music and postmodern theory	p. 174
Lawrence Grossberg	Rock, territorialization and power	p. 358
Mica Nava	Consumerism reconsidered: buying and power	p. 157
Davide Rowe	'That misery of stringer's clichés': sports writing	p. 77
Tim Rowse	'Interpretive possibilities': Aboriginal men and clothing	p. 1
Paul Rutten	Local popular music on the national and international markets	p. 294
Roger Silverstone, Eric Hirsch and David Morley	Listening to a long conversation: an ethnographic approach to the study of information and communication technologies in the home	p. 204
Will Straw	Systems of articulation, logics of change: communities and scenes in popular music	p. 368

Paul Théberge	Musicians' magazines in the 1980s: the creation of a community and a consumer market	p. 270
McKenzie Wark	Fashioning the future: fashion, clothing, and the manufacturing of post-Fordist culture	p. 61
Janice Winship	The impossibility of *Best*: enterprise meets domesticity in the practical women's magazines of the 1980s	p. 131
Robert Wright	'Gimme Shelter': observations on cultural protectionism and the recording industry in Canada	p. 306

Kites and reviews

Patrice Fleck	Pornotopia?	p. 389
John Frow	Face value?	p. 393
Rosalind Gill	Radio Ga-ga?	p. 113
Philip Hayward	Desire caught by its tale: the unlikely return of the merman in Madonna's *Cherish*	p. 98
Stevi Jackson	Organizational sexuality	p. 122
Klaus Bruhn Jensen	Cultural Studies 101	p. 107
Shaun Richards	Liberating the audience	p. 246
Mary Yelanjian	Rhythms of consumption	p. 91

OXFORD UNIVERSITY PRESS

Sexual Dissidence
Augustine to Wilde, Freud to Foucault
JONATHAN DOLLIMORE

Jonathan Dollimore brilliantly links writers and cultural critics from Shakespeare to Gide and Genet, and from St Augustine to Fanon and Monique Wittig in this wide-ranging study of the status of homosexuality in literature and society from the early modern period to the present.

0 19 811225 4, 400 pages, Clarendon Press £35.00
0 19 811269 6, Oxford Paperbacks £9.95

Sister's Choice
Tradition and Change in American Women's Writing
ELAINE SHOWALTER

This study argues that post-colonial as well as feminist literary theory can help us understand the complex forms of American women's writing, and the way that 'women's culture' intersects with other cultural forms.

0 19 812383 3, 216 pages, 7 halftones, Clarendon Press £22.50

Women: A Cultural Review
Volume 2: Issue 3
Edited by **ISOBEL ARMSTRONG** and **HELEN CARR**

The theme of this issue is Culture and Ethnicity and articles include Lola Young on bel hooks, Jean Franco on Latin American women, and Southall Black Sisters on the Danger of Multiculturalism.

0 19 922093 X, 100 pages, paper covers £6.95
December 1991

Marvelous Possessions
The Wonder of the New World
STEPHEN GREENBLATT

Stephen Greenblatt's innovative readings of travel narratives, judicial documents, and official reports explore the way in which Europeans of the late middle ages and early modern period represented non-European peoples and took possession of their lands, in particular the New World.

0 19 812382 5, 216 pages, 8 pp plates, 6 halftones, Clarendon Press £22.50

The Flesh Made Word
Female Figures and Women's Bodies
HELENA MICHIE

Looks at how women's bodies are portrayed in a variety of Victorian literary and non-literary genres, from paintings, poems, and novels, to etiquette books and pornography.

0 19 506081 4, 188 pages, 5 halftones, paper covers, OUP USA £9.95

For more details, please contact Jason Freeman, Oxford University Press, Walton Street, Oxford OX2 6DP

POLYTECHNIC OF EAST LONDON

MA and Diploma in Cultural Studies: History and Theory
(full-time and part-time)

Post-structuralism and critiques of ethnocentrism; feminism and subjectivity; psychoanalysis and Marxism ... recent developments in cultural theory have been breathtaking. But how do these theories affect how we think historically?

The MA and Diploma are constructed around this central question. The course investigates current theories of culture and explores issues such as historical imagination and popular memory; historical fictions; different genres of historical narrative; everyday histories; and discourses of Empire and nation.

We are looking for students prepared to work intensively as part of a larger intellectual project, contributing their own research in both core and options. Candidates with any background in the social sciences or humanities are welcome to apply. In exceptional circumstances people who have no first degree will be considered.

Course team: Sally Alexander, Andrew Blake, Robert Chase, Steven Fielding, Catherine Hall, Mica Nava, Alan O'Shea, Kenneth Parker, Bill Schwarz, Couze Venn.

MPhil/PhD supervision and BA(Hons) also offered.

Further information and application forms available from:
The MA Course Secretary
Department of Cultural Studies
Polytechnic of East London
Longbridge Road
Dagenham, Essex RM8 2AS
Tel. 081-849 3545

The Polytechnic is an Equal Opportunities Employer

For Product Safety Concerns and Information please contact our EU
representative GPSR@taylorandfrancis.com
Taylor & Francis Verlag GmbH, Kaufingerstraße 24, 80331 München, Germany

www.ingramcontent.com/pod-product-compliance
Lightning Source LLC
Chambersburg PA
CBHW052050300426
44117CB00012B/2056